Creating High Performers

7 Questions to Ask Your Direct Reports

By
William Dann

Foreword by Ken Blanchard
Author of The One Minute Manager

Creating High Performers: 7 Questions to Ask Your Direct Reports
Published through Growth Press, LLC

Interior Book Design and Layout by
www.integrativeink.com

ISBN: 978-0-9909440-0-3

Growth Press, LLC
911 W. Eighth Ave., Suite 205
Anchorage, AK 99501

GROWTH PRESS

Table of Contents

Foreword v

Acknowledgements vii

1. Introduction..1

2. The Leadership Context...7

3. The Two Types of Supervisory Problems.................17

4. Why This Matters..25

5. The 7 Questions 29

    Question #1 – Expectations 33

    Question #2 – Good Performance 43

    Question #3 – Feedback..................................47

    Question #4 – Authority.................................53

    Question #5 – Timely Decisions....................59

    Question #6 – Resources.................................63

    Question #7 – Credit......................................73

6. The Underlying Principle of Fairness....................79

7. Putting the 7 Questions to Work.........................85

8. Troubleshooting..99

9. Some Final Thoughts 113

Appendix..115

FOREWORD

FOR A LONG time, I've been interested in the subject of managing people's performance. To me, there have always been three parts of that process: *performance planning*, where you set goals and establish coaching strategies; d*ay-to-day coaching*, where you follow through on what you agreed upon in order to help people win by accomplishing their goals; and *performance evaluation*, where you assess how well the person has performed over time. Of these three aspects, which is typically the most time consuming for managers? Performance evaluation. This tends to be the time when they have to sit down and fill out forms on each of their people and sort them into a normal distribution format—only a few win, a few have to lose, and the rest are considered average. Or, even worse, they may have to rank order their people. Bill Dann is condemns this process, and so am I.

It has always amazed me how very few organizations do extensive performance planning where clear goals are set. They're even worse when it comes to how little day-to-day coaching goes on.

I always ask managers in my training sessions "How many of you hire losers? Do you say, 'We lost some of our best losers last year, so let's hire some new ones to fill those low spots'? Of course you don't! You either hire winners—people who already have good performance records in their position; or you hire potential winners—people whom you believe you can train to be high performers. Obviously, you don't hire on a normal distribution curve."

Bill Dann and I wonder why every leader or manager wouldn't want every person to potentially win—to be a high performer who gets As? Yet, to do that, managers have to talk to their people. That's why I love Bill's book. He introduces 7 questions you can use to partner with your people for better performance.

Peter Drucker always said, "Nothing good ever happens by accident." If you want something good to happen, you have to put some structure around it. If you want your people to perform well, meet and talk with them about how they are performing. Use Bill Dann's good questions and I guarantee not only that you will become a better leader/manager, but that your people will become better performers.

Thanks Bill, you're the best.

Ken Blanchard
Co-Founder, The Ken Blanchard Companies
Coauthor of *The One Minute Manager*® and *Leading at a Higher Level*

ACKNOWLEDGEMENTS

COMING TO THE belief that I have something worthwhile to share has taken awhile. I would not have taken this leap without the encouragement of many people close to me. Some of you were students, some were co-workers, some were clients, some were friends and some were loved ones. There are too many of you to mention. But, there are a few of you that I must name and acknowledge.

First is my friend and mentor, Ken Blanchard. In addition to being an inspirational human being, Ken clarified leadership for me. He defined it in understandable terms, called leaders to their true responsibility and challenged us to never lose faith in those who work for and support us. He has provided the tools to be able to execute what is a complex duty. Most importantly, Ken has lived his life in integrity with his beliefs and teachings. His own success is a testament to that integrity and to the wisdom of his teachings.

Second, I want to acknowledge my first business partner, Jeannette Morton. Before I even had been exposed to Ken's model, she demonstrated the two keys to being a Situational Leader, "flexibility" and "effectiveness." At the time, I was a bleeding heart liberal and a locked-in Supportive Leader while believing I could love all those who worked for me into a higher performance. Jeannette demonstrated that for some non-performers a firm, unbending demand for change was the correct leadership course. She showed the courage to practice from her convictions, despite being criticized by some as being cruel. Her heart bled when being stern, but just not in front of the employee. She practiced tough love and demonstrated to me its efficacy.

Third, I want to thank Bill Bicknell, M.D., who was a lifelong mentor and an early patron of my work as a manager and teacher. Most recently, he had been a persistent cheerleader for me to publish what I have come to learn and write about in newsletters and blogs. Bill passed away not long ago, and at that point I committed myself to finish this book that had been rattling around in my head for years.

Next is Andrea Garrels with whom I have been blessed to have worked for over twenty years. Throughout our time together, she has steered me straight when I wandered and she forced me to be clear when I wasn't. Her first edits were invaluable and her enthusiasm for the project kept me motivated.

I owe a great deal to Gerry Faust, Bill Popp, Doug Saunders and Steve McComb for their encouragement after early reads that moved me forward.

Stephanee Killen and the team at Integrative Ink were invaluable guides through the publication process.

Lastly, I want to thank my wife Jenny Alowa for always believing in me and encouraging me to "go for it," as she says.

1. INTRODUCTION

How I Got Here

I HAVE BEEN challenged as a leader for nearly forty years and have taught and coached leadership for over thirty years. The fact that there are countless books on the subject can be attributed to true leadership being difficult and, in my view, scarce.

how is true leadership defined?

As human beings we are immensely diverse and often struggle with life. Thus, it is of little wonder that the aspect of leadership that involves helping others to reach their full potential while they contribute to organizational results is daunting and, at times, discouraging. There are many variables, no magic formula as well as high risk for misunderstandings and falling short of the mark.

My own journey as a leader, alongside the work with students and coaching CEO's, has led to a fascination with the subject.

I have been blessed by several life experiences that have contributed to the writing of this book.

First, early in my career, I became involved in the War on Poverty. I was asked to found and develop a regional health corporation in the "bush" of Alaska whose purpose was to bring self-determination and improved health outcomes to Alaskan Natives by having them design and implement their own programs. In striving to fulfill that purpose, I hired and worked with many for whom the job was their first. They were thrust into a work environment with highly trained professionals where the stakes were literally life and death. That journey included putting individuals into supervisory roles for the first time. I was able to see firsthand what the challenges were going to be, what worked in developing leaders and what did not. I gained insight into some fundamental principles that I don't believe I would have gained anywhere else. It was immensely instructive.

Second, in the mid-70's I connected with Ken Blanchard, co-author of the <u>One Minute Manager</u>[1] author of numerous other successful books and developer of the Situational Leadership II® model[2]. Ken's leadership theory and principles remain the foundation for my own learning and for the teaching of others. Ken inspires leaders to see the innate goodness and potential in their fellow man and to manifest that potential in the workplace. Ken and I share a common purpose line in this regard.

Third, I was asked in the early 80's to teach management at the Boston University School of Public Health to Master's candidates and to public health management certificate attendees who came from throughout the developing world. Experiences with both groups affirmed that I had learned some basic principles of management and supervision that weren't in the literature of the time and were universal across cultures.

Lastly, clients and students throughout my consulting career have encouraged me to publish my learning's, for which I am forever grateful.

My Intended Contribution

As a basic primer on leadership, I commend you to Ken Blanchard's Situational Leadership II® Model. This model is unmatched in its clarity and ease of use. Ken calls leaders to a purpose of developing "winners" and offers easy to use methods to achieve that end. Use of this model facilitates supervisors and subordinates dialoguing, in a non-threatening way, on how each can contribute to achieving the employee's full potential.

---

1   Blanchard, Ken & Johnson, Spencer, <u>The One Minute Manager</u>, William Morrow, 1982
2   Blanchard, Ken, <u>Leadership and The One Minute Manager</u> (updated edition), 2013, William Morrow

Enabling an employee to reach his or her potential requires commitment and discipline. Many leaders struggle with completing annual evaluations, let alone training subordinates on new skills, coaching them to proficiency and supporting them through ongoing feedback and validation.

However, in my own journey and that of those I have trained & coached, the greatest challenge comes with confronting and effectively dealing with employees who underperform. The tendency is to either hope matters improve or to actively demonstrate compassion in order to encourage improvement. I, and others I have worked with, grind for months on end on questions like: "What else should I do?" "What did I fail to do?" "What did I do wrong?" "Should I talk to him/her?" "When will it turn around?" Spinning on these questions rather than confronting the poor performance didn't work for me and wasn't working for others.

The question of when and how to manage underperformance was consistently the leading question of my students and those I was coaching. So, I set out on a quest to find answers and to develop tools to help others with these questions.

The Two Types of Problems Can't do vs. won't do

Ken defines two types of problems that supervisors face in developing employees: Can't Do vs. Won't Do problems. Can't Do problems are solved through effective action by the leader. Actions include goal setting, coaching, mentoring and supporting good results to build confidence. Can't Do problems are the responsibility of the leader.

Won't Do problems can only be solved by the employee, who must first take ownership of the problem. In Won't Do problems, the employee has the direction, skills and confidence needed but is choosing to not perform. Once a Won't Do problem is owned by the employee, the leader can assist, but the shift in ownership must come first. _Bottom 20%?_

This book is intended as a guide to help you diagnose whether you are experiencing a Can't Do or Won't Do problem, and then develop an action plan to handle it. It is intended to break the cycle of needlessly blaming yourself for shortcomings as a leader in instances where the shortcomings are those of the employee and are his/her responsibility to address.

In addition, I seek to improve your performance as a supervisor in those instances where the employee's performance is going fine, but there remains unrealized potential. This is accomplished by raising the quality, specificity and value of performance conversations between supervisor and subordinate. Those conversations will be covered in depth throughout the book.

What I hope to offer supervisors with this book is **a)** a means by which you can discover the specifics as to how you can better contribute to optimum performance of your direct reports, and **b)** to put an end to the agony over what to do with subordinate underperformance. It is a guide on how to spot the source of the underperformance, gain clarity on what you vs. your subordinate may be responsible for and to take effective action early on.

The book is organized around a set of diagnostic questions that I refer to as the "7 Questions." Several of the questions I attribute to Ken Blanchard's teachings. I have added a few questions from my own journey as well. I devote a chapter to each question and attempt to illuminate its importance through a true story. The names in the stories have been changed to protect the victims of my own failures as each lesson and the question arising from it are sourced in a failure from my leadership journey or observing the successes of other leaders.

How to Use This Book

I would suggest that you read through the book in its entirety to become familiar with the overall approach, including how to introduce the conversation around the 7 Questions and when to use them.

Prior to having an initial conversation with one of your employees, think through why you are using the tool, how you are going to introduce the conversation and the 7 Questions themselves. Look over Chapter 6 on "The Underlying Principle of Fairness" to determine whether you need to explore if fairness exists or not. I have suggested questions to help make that judgment as well. Lastly, go back through the chapters on each question and decide what follow-on questions you want to employ to get clarity as to why you may have gotten a "no" on a given question or what you need to do to get to a "yes." There are several suggestions for additional questions in each chapter. Following these steps, you should be ready to **a)** make any needed revisions to the "contract" with your employee and **b)** develop a specific leadership action plan to either move the employee along to their potential or get them to take responsibility for their unacceptable performance.

2. The Leadership Context

BEFORE I DIVE into the 7 Questions and how to use them to bring about improved performance, I want to set a bit of context. The 7 Questions are used by supervisors to get into meaningful conversation with their direct reports. So, a bit of this "context setting" is to get clear on the roles of a leader and supervisor, some common supervisory problems and the importance of good communication. Then, I end this chapter with a look at what I hope the 7 Questions do *not* become, i.e., the dreaded annual evaluation. Armed with this context as our base, we can easily move into the questions and their application.

So let's begin.

Role of a Leader

Leadership happens at all levels in an organization. However, it takes on different forms and significances at the various levels.

At the top of the organization, the leader is charged with three principle responsibilities: **1)** clear direction, i.e., assuring that the organization has a strategy that ensures future viability, **2)** safety, i.e., keeping the work environment safe for those working in it, and **3)** control, i.e., defining how the organization should operate and then assuring that it does. Fulfilling these responsibilities gives employees faith in the ability and integrity of their leaders. If any one of these is absent then employees feel uncertain about their future or unsafe.

Although the leaders at the top of the organization fulfill the first three responsibilities, leaders at all levels within the organization share some responsibility and should be contributing to all these leadership elements. Strategy is not the sole domain of the CEO. Those lowest in the organization are often the best source of information about customer needs and level of satisfaction. This is vital information for the development of sound strategy. In high performing organizations, leaders at all levels participate in strategy development.

Front-line supervisors and their employees know best how to design processes to get defined results efficiently and consistently. The front-line play a vital role in defining and maintaining order by designing sound methods or processes. Inefficiency or inconsistency of results constitutes disorder.

At all levels of the organization, leaders are charged with a fourth responsibility, which is that of developing the full potential of their employees. This responsibility is often called "supervision." The demands and methods for supervision are the same at each level. The variation lies in the abilities and confidence of the employees (what Blanchard calls Development Level) and not in the level on the organizational chart or functional area.

Understanding the elements of leadership at various levels can help put the 7 Questions that are the subject of this book in the proper context. Let's look at them a little more closely.

Elements of Leadership

1. Direction

In essence, followers look to leaders for a strategy that assures future viability and prosperity. Strategy involves assessing the outside environment and defining any needed changes that meet opportunities/threats, thus assuring that the products or services of the organization (be they for-profit or non-profit) are considered value-added to paying customers, donors, or grantors. At best, it means defining and executing on innovations that keep you ahead of your competitors. The strategy needs to be clear to and supported by followers who understand how their own efforts contribute to future viability. Belief in the future, a sense of mission and faith in leadership is the outcome of effective direction.

The distinction here is that at the top of the house, direction really entails strategy. In supervision that occurs at all levels, direction means defining priorities, setting goals and teaching/coaching on task completion.

I think it can but isn't a requirement. In the largest companies, CEOs don't have time to teach/coach. That role is generally saved for subordinates

2. Safety

Employees need freedom from external threats in order to contribute their full potential. Safety entails an absence of political intrigue, lawsuits, regulatory threats and abusive management practices. At best, it means the community views the organization as a good citizen. Employees feel free to innovate, to be honest in their communications and to engage with management to solve problems. Alternatively, an atmosphere of treachery will suppress these contributions.

not sure the same thing

Important & crucial but not always present

3. Order

At its essence, order means assuring that what is intended is in fact carried out. Order consists of both clarity and consistency. It means that effective routines are established and there is sufficient certainty in the workplace. Employees are not anxious about random changes that are disruptive. Processes are clear. Lines of authority and communication are clear. Rules are clear and consistently enforced. Employees know their own responsibilities and what they can expect from others they must team with in order to produce the needed results. Productivity is the basis of morale. Order versus confusion is vital to productivity. The tough part is ensuring that all these policies and processes are adhered to. Without it, leadership integrity is eroded, cynicism germinates and the organization underperforms.

4. Supervision

At all levels, those charged with supervision responsibility are charged with bringing to fruition the full potential of their employees.

When using the definition of supervision previously defined. You can supervise without developing. You don't have to supervise to develop

Another early influence in my thinking on management was Louis Allen. In his self-published book, The Louis Allen Principles of Professional Management[3], he made the distinction between "technical work" (delivering results to customers) and "management work" (delivering results for customers through others). In Allen's model, "management work" consists of planning, organizing, leading and controlling. Essentially, these are the same elements that are described above. Allen sees management work as being done at all levels of the organization. At the top, a leader's time should be spent almost entirely on management work, whereas at the bottom the time may be more of an even split between technical and management work. For example, the supervisor in a hospital laboratory may be performing some tests in addition to planning work, supervising and the like.

The distinction Allen makes between the two types of work was a real "aha" moment for me. What I saw was that "management work" was overhead. It adds to the cost of the product or service. If an organization can manage effectively with less investment in management work, it will be more profitable or be able to deliver more service. Then I saw that if I was doing management work, but that work did not result in better results from my employees, then I was not adding value. I was purely an expense that added no value to the customer or the organization. It was at that point that I took supervision much more seriously and focused my learning on the question of, how can I do a better job of unleashing the potential of those who work with me? This became a lifelong journey of learning for me.

What Louis Allen found in his research is the consistent presence of what he called "the management gap." The "gap" is the difference between the percentage of a manager's time that goes into "management work" versus the actual amount of time needed to do it effectively. Allen attributed this to what he called "the principle of technical priority," which means that managers will chose to do technical work rather than management work when given a choice. The result is those reporting to that manager will underperform relative to their potential.

---

3 Louis A. Allen Associates Inc., 1969

I have consistently found this same phenomena, i.e., supervisors don't supervise. They don't effectively direct, coach, encourage or mentor. Why? Management work is harder than technical work. Human beings are more difficult to deal with and supervisors lack tools and training. There is a host of reasons why.

Many people that I have worked with attribute the "gap" to lack of time, but my take is that it is lack of commitment. They have not had the "aha" moment yet. So, those of you who feel that you don't have time for supervision should consider the fact that you only add value to the organization as a supervisor if you bring about a higher level of performance with direct reports than would have been the case were you not supervising. If you are not spending time striving to move your employees toward their potential, then how are you adding value to the organization?

Supervisors don't often think in these terms. It is a subtle, but important difference to distinguish between "How I can do more to get more" vs. "How can I get more"; "more" being a higher level of performance from employees. The key lies in understanding what the supervisor vs. employee is responsible for in achieving good performance. The 7 Questions are intended to aid you in gaining that understanding and acting on it.

The Importance of Communication

In any relationship, communication is critical, including that of a supervisor and employee. Communication is the route to mutual understanding and agreement. Miscommunication or lack of communication leads to misunderstanding and disagreement. The level of understanding and agreement largely determines how productive and rewarding a working relationship will be. Communication is the essential key to the effectiveness of the 7 Questions.

Work is a team endeavor. You won't have a real team unless there is agreement on what to do, how to do it and the like. You won't progress unless you can agree upon the existence of and solution for problems. You simply can't get there if communication is absent or ineffective.

The more one feels like what they have to say will be understood; the more one is willing to communicate. Have you ever tried to talk to someone who clearly wasn't interested or listening? You won't try that for very long and you are not likely to initiate a conversation the next time you meet them.

Similarly, the greater the level of agreement, then the greater the willingness to share what is true, even if there is potential for disagreement. If there is generally agreement, then disagreements are not threatening. If I know that someone has a similar view of the world, e.g. Democrat with another Democrat or Republican with another Republican, Catholic with another Catholic etc., then it becomes easier to express our differences of opinion. In short, if one feels as if what is said will be understood and there won't be a negative reaction, then there is a willingness to communicate further. If not, there is a tendency to hold back communication.

You can see that these two elements are interdependent. The more I communicate, the greater the chance that I will discover that I am in agreement with someone else. The more I am in agreement with someone else, the more likely I am to communicate.

I once asked my father, late in his life, why it was that he would not communicate more with me. He responded that he had never been a good communicator and was not about to try and be one at this late stage in his life. My guess is that his efforts to be understood in the past had been frustrated. He didn't want to suffer another loss.

Each time one makes an attempt to be understood and is unsuccessful, another barrier to being open and honest is created. Since so many of the employees you work with have likely had challenges similar to my father, then achieving high quality two-way communication is difficult, indeed.

Therefore, the first hurdle in using the 7 Questions is convincing your employee that you are genuinely interested in learning what is true for them and that discovering where your views differ is the key to improving your working relationships and fulfilling their potential. In short, being honest and having a healthy exchange of ideas is the first step to bettering the work experience for both of you. If you make it clear that you see your job as assuring that a good work experience happens and that you intend to make the needed changes, then this should generate an openness that the employee has rarely, if ever, experienced.

Begin the conversation by asking a question that expresses your genuine interest in hearing from the employee, i.e., invite a response and you are likely to get one. Continuing to ask genuine questions will ultimately generate the employee's interest in learning what is true from your perspective. In the mind of the employee, the thought is, "Gee, all this interest in me, maybe I should now show some interest in what he/she sees." For example, if I were to ask you several questions about how you and members of your family were doing, eventually you would begin asking about my family. It just feels like the right thing to do when someone expresses genuine interest in you.

The 7 Questions focus on what is vital in your relationship with your subordinate. After responding to a few of your questions, you will generate employee interest in learning what is true for you. They will want to know, "How are you seeing my performance?" "Where could I do better?" "What else could I contribute that would be valuable?" This two-way conversation has the potential to be much more productive than the normal performance review, which is largely a one-way communication.

The 7 Questions can set the table for an honest and productive exchange and development of a game plan for improvement by both parties. What normally would have been a very difficult conversation will now become much easier.

An Example

A CEO I was coaching put this principle to work. I had suggested that as a leader it was vital to first seek to understand before seeking to be understood. He was able to see how important this was. He also saw that both he and his management team lacked understanding of what was really going on inside the company because they weren't listening enough. He counseled his management team to monitor their communications with employees, i.e. how many words they were speaking vs. how many they were listening to. His rule of thumb, "For every word you communicate, I want you to listen to five words." Putting this to work shifted how employees perceived management. Top down, one-way communication was replaced by a sense that management was there to serve. The culture inside the organization improved dramatically as a result.

The Annual Evaluation

The annual evaluation is regarded as the event at which the most honest, in-depth conversations should take place. It is the point at which supervisor and employee take stock of how the working relationship is progressing.

There are real differences of opinion regarding the benefit of the annual performance evaluations as it is most commonly practiced today. My experience is that as they are usually practiced, performance evaluations don't add much value and can actually do damage. They are intimidating to most, while being unfair and subjective to many. I am going to suggest that periodic and regular conversations utilizing the 7 Questions replace this annual, anxiety-provoking event.

The annual evaluation often doesn't deliver what is intended, that is, a means to improve and reward performance. One of the reasons for this is that the evaluations are often tied to changes in compensation. Compensation becomes the focus rather than the improvement of performance.

Years ago, I was visiting with a friend of mine who was a partner in a large accounting firm. He had just returned from an annual partner retreat in Hawaii at which, among other things, decisions were made on the annual bonuses for employees. He was complaining that after the bonuses were handed out there was turmoil and complaints throughout the ranks. His take on it all was, "Well, if I am going to get that much grief from handing out money, maybe I should just keep it." I advised that it may not be the correct solution. I then inquired as to how they went about assigning bonuses. It was clear that there were no real standards and that the so-called standards that were used weren't made known in advance. In short, the process was arbitrary and capricious. The employees saw that they were in a game with unknown rules and that they couldn't win. So, the bonus program sowed discontent rather than raised morale. Not uncommon.

A Word About Rewards

Work is a team sport. Everyone's performance is dependent upon the work of others to some degree. Those who choose to go it alone in pursuit of, say, the highest sales totals are often destructive to the group as a whole. The sales superstars withhold their secrets, hoard their leads, give away profit to make the sale, etc. So, when we focus on the individual in establishing rewards, it can lead to sub-optimizing vs. accelerating performance.

I am a fan of a group incentive allocated based on salary. That is, a certain percentage of profit or increased performance/reduced cost, (which always equates to money in some fashion even in non-profits), is allocated as a bonus or profit share. Divide the amount of the total budget for bonuses by the total payroll cost and that determines the percent of bonuses that go to each employee. This is fair provided the salary structure is fair and supervisors are dealing effectively with poor performers. As long as everyone is viewed generally as doing their best to contribute, then this system is fair. I have just never seen a situation where rewarding individuals has been perceived as fair. Team-based rewards may also be perceived as unfair if there are instances in which underperforming ("won't do") employees are not being dealt with and are being carried by others.

An Alternative Approach

Well, if we move to a methodology based on team rewards, then what about the annual evaluation? I suggest shifting to set this up as a semi-annual conversation about how working conditions, effectiveness, productivity and supervision for each employee can be improved. It is here that the 7 Questions can perform well.

Making this shift takes much of the pressure off. The annual judgment day now becomes the annual conversation (keep in mind that I think this should be done at least semi-annually). We now have a dialogue on how both parties, supervisor and employee, can improve. With compensation out of the picture, the conversation is easier and more valuable.

This, then, is the context from which the 7 Questions flourish. Effective leadership and sound communication, coupled with an understanding of the challenges that various employees may present will lay the groundwork. So, let's get to the questions themselves.

My hope with this book is that it will provide greater certainty as to how to execute your responsibilities as a supervisor and with that certainty, you will close the "management gap" and realize the potential of your workforce.

3. THE TWO TYPES OF SUPERVISORY PROBLEMS

BLANCHARD HAS SAID, there are two categories of problems in supervision, a "Can't Do" and a "Won't Do" problem. Can't Do problems are the responsibility of supervisors to solve. Won't Do problems are the responsibility of employees to solve.

The challenge for supervisors is to determine which type of problem exists and then take effective action on it. Without clarity on which problem exists, an effective plan of correction cannot be developed or carried out. There will not be proper actions in that plan or the proper assigning of responsibility for action.

The 7 Questions are intended to help you make the call; "Am I, as supervisor, responsible for this problem (Can't Do)?" or "Should I be holding the employee responsible for the problem (Won't Do)?" I will go into further detail on handling these two categories of problems in Chapter 8, but for now, here is a quick explanation of each as well as issues that fall on the border.

1.) Can't Do Problems

"Can't Do" problems arise because the employee has not been given the tools for success. Can't Do problems can arise because of one more of the following reasons:

- Lack of pre-requisite skills and experience.
  A faulty hiring process can result in an employee not having a chance of succeeding. While it is true that on the job training

can be effective, unless an employee has the basic skills and experience to be successful, they feel as if and are in fact set up for failure. Especially in supervisory positions, it is challenging to recover from a poor start in which employees feel as if they have to train their supervisor.

- **Lack of clarity on responsibilities**
  Lack of or conflicting direction as to products, priorities or deadlines. The lack of clarity can arise because of 1) multiple sources of supervision or responsibilities being shared by more than one position, both are organizational structure issues, or 2) inconsistent messages from a supervisor. In short, the employee can't do it because they don't know what it is.

- **Lack of understanding of the supervisor's standard for a good work product**
  The employee may bring the skills and experience required for a given responsibility but they don't know your standard for that responsibility or work product. Thus, again, they can't do it because you have not informed them of what it is.

- **Lack of or unclear rules and procedures**
  Each organization has its own culture. The culture can be thought of as a set of norms of behavior. Sometimes these are unwritten or not communicated and the new employee can stick out like a sore thumb, e.g. wear the wrong clothes, engage in type of humor or other behavior that is frowned on, regard time and engaging socially differently from the norm. Again, the employee can't do it your way because they don't know what your way is. I am familiar with a highly successful health care provider that requires all new employees to go through a one-week introduction to "the way" at that organization, i.e. its core beliefs and operating principles, how to operate in a team setting etc. This would be the ultimate cure for this Can't Do problem.

- Lack of feedback

  The first time an employee takes a shot at doing what they understand is expected in the way in which it is expected, they need feedback that they did or did not get it right. Without the feedback, they are likely to modify their method or product the next time out again due to lack of certainty about what to do. The uncertainty arising from lack of feedback can lead to reduced productivity as well as inconsistent quality of work product.

  In relaying each of the reasons for Can't Do problems arising I have written about new employees, but these Can't Do problems can arise well into the term of employment because of lack of supervision. Also, as Blanchard points out in his SL II® model, each time you assign an employee a new responsibility or task, you need to become more directive in your leadership style. In short, you have to get "Yes" answers anew to the 7 Questions.

2) Confidence Problems

On the borderline between Can't Do and Won't Do is the employee's inability to operate independently, initiate change or take risks. A lack of confidence or fear of failure can be the source. This could arise from the employee's read of the supervisor, i.e. making a mistake will bring a strong reprimand. Or, it could be sourced in the employee's history and mental state at any given time. If fear of repercussions from their supervisor is the source, then the supervisor owns the problem. If it is the employee's history or mental state, the employee owns it.

As an example, at a welcoming party for a new office manager I once hired, I became curious as to why the new employee was so distant when we had made such a great connection during the hiring process. When I inquired, he responded with, "You are now my boss," I replied, "Yes, that is the hat that I wear, but I am me, we are in a social setting, so why the change and avoidance of me." He responded with "You now have control over my life." I learned that he had been the victim of punishing, arbitrary supervision in the past and was anxious about starting work with an unknown boss. We worked it out quickly, but had we not, he would have avoided making decisions and his performance would have fallen well short of his potential, which was enormous.

In this example, there was a shared responsibility. The employee brought in baggage that could have negatively impacted his performance or the speed of his development. In a sense, he was responsible to make that known and certainly controlled whether or not he would come to trust me as his supervisor. My responsibility was to spot this caution and then to take positive steps to overcome it.

A supervisor can contribute to overcoming these barriers, but ultimately the employee must own them if they are to be overcome. Encouragement and two-way communication can go a long way here, but ultimately the employee has to make the leap. This is rather like taking the training wheels off your child's bicycle. Ultimately, you have to let go. If the child shuts down and refuses to take the risk, there is little the parent can do.

When there is turnover in a position, research shows it takes 6-9 months to regain the level of performance in that position. The critical variable here is how well the supervisor does in filling the gaps, i.e. eliminating the Can't Do problems. Most employee orientation programs are deficient and many supervisors complain that they simply don't have enough time to perform good supervision.

Filling the gaps in training, direction and coaching, followed by feedback and rewards for performance solve Can't Do problems. The 7 Questions will help you diagnose which element is deficient and then dialogue about the specific misunderstandings, skill deficiencies, questions that need to be addressed, etc. Employing these questions should enable you to shorten the time required to get a new employee up to speed.

3) Won't Do Problems

Won't Do problems arise because the employee consciously or sub-consciously is choosing to not perform as directed. That is, if you have answered fully all of the 7 Questions, then poor performance becomes an employee choice on some level.

The challenge is that employee's with such problems will mask them. They appear to always be busy, engaged, committed, and hard-working. But, at the end of the day, they aren't producing a product or not the one that you want. You don't press them because they seem to be "my best employee". The product that they do produce is often con-fusion. When pressed, they state that they didn't understand or were confused. Further, they sow confusion among co-workers so as to take away the ability to distinguish the Won't Do employee from those who are being productive. Teams containing such employees are frequently in disarray. Won't Do employees and those working with them often have high rates of using sick days.

When pressed, using the 7 Questions or other questions, Won't Do employees will speak in generalities about problems or barriers to their producing what you want. The end result here is that the supervisor won't have the information needed to solve the problem because the problem can never get defined.

So, the only way to really diagnose a Won't Do problem is by a) looking at statistics that bear out a lack of production and b) employing the 7 Questions but finding that in the end you have nothing tangible to correct as supervisor. That is, you have qualified "yes" answers to all the questions. So, you are left with a mystery. Well, there is no mystery here. It's a Won't Do problem.

Won't Do problems arise for a number of reasons among them:

1) the employee has lost motivation (or never had it)

2) the employee is seeking revenge or to even the score for some perceived injustice (e.g. passed over for promotion)

3) the employee no longer supports the mission

4) the employee is experiencing a personal problem (e.g. divorce, addiction)

Ultimately, the employee owns these problems. They are Won't Do in nature. The circumstances may be understandable, even tragic, but this should not prompt the supervisor to take responsibility for such problems. The supervisor can't solve them. He can only aid their solution by the employee.

Won't Do problems may justify lenience in approving leave or time off for counseling, even investing in some form of help; but they do not justify continuing to not meet performance standards. They only explain them.

The hurdle that well-meaning supervisors need to overcome is putting the welfare of the team and organization first at some point.

Ken Blanchard's original research that was the basis for the Situational Leadership® model was on parenting. Ken then likened growing employees to growing children. The challenge in both situations is gaining clarity as to whether a problem is due to deficient parenting or the willful choice of the child. Loving the child makes it difficult to harshly judge and punish a child. The same is true for the supervisor concerned about and committed to his employees. But, lack of discipline, when warranted, is detrimental to both children and employees.

Furthermore, not disciplining employees with Won't Do problems erodes the standing of the leader. It represents a failure to provide both order and safety in the form of fairness. An employee not meeting standards means that other employees must endure some measure of chaos and must pick up added work for which they are usually not recognized or rewarded.

The 7 Questions should give you greater clarity as to whether you have done all you can and the employee owns the problem you both face. Having the employee agree that you have, indeed, done all that you can, should strengthen your resolve to confront the employee's choice to not perform.

4. WHY THIS MATTERS

Anna

My first day at work in Boston I was given a general orientation, told which functions within the Department were to be my responsibility and then shown to my office. On the way down the hall from the Commissioner's office, the Director of Administration offered some advice. "You will be sharing two secretaries with two other executives. One of them is Anna. Anna has been here 26 years and hasn't worked a lick in the last 20 or so. My advice is that you simply ignore that she exists because you won't get any work out of her and you can't fire her." As I entered the suite of offices, Anna sat at a desk immediately to the left. I recognized her without an introduction because she looked totally miserable. Her complexion was gray in color, her eyes sunken with deep circles beneath them and she had a sour look on her face. Her desk showed no signs of activity and her typewriter (yes, it was that long ago) still had its cover on.

I said, "Hello," then moved on to be introduced to the others. The phone rang shortly thereafter, and Anna ignored it. She left it to Linda, the other secretary, to do that.

I didn't make a whole lot of the incident at first, but after days of walking by Anna repeatedly and seeing no signs of productivity, life, communication, humor or enjoyment; it began to wear on me. Furthermore, it was apparent that I was going to be buried with work and was going to need real assistance.

So, after about a week, I asked Anna to come into my office and chat. I think she was startled by the request. I began as follows,

"Anna what they told me about you is that you have been here 26 years, that you haven't done any real work for the last 20, and that I should not expect that to change or try and make it so. Well, I'm just not comfortable assuming that based on what other people tell me, so I would like to hear from you about that."

Anna's eyes came alive and were riveted on me. Something I had not seen since I got there. Anna began, and almost immediately the tears began flowing. "When I started here, I worked hard and no one seemed to notice or care. So, after several years I decided to stop working and see what happened. Well, nothing happened. They didn't seem to care about that either, so I just stopped working and that's where I have been ever since." I was stunned. I responded with, "Well, Anna, I do care. I don't want you sitting here being miserable and not feeling productive. Besides, I have lots of work to do and could really use the help."

Anna's backbone stiffened and her face came alive. She said, "Well, then, let's get to work." She marched out of my office, went to her desk and uncovered her typewriter, then came back in with a steno pad to ask me what I needed done. As she came to my office, she entreated Linda to get to work.

Thereafter, not only was Anna going back to her productive self, but her entire physical appearance and demeanor in the office changed. The scowl was gone. She was gruff by nature, but her humor came out and she genuinely enjoyed herself. She would regularly growl at Linda to get to work. She became my protector. Better yet, she made me fresh baklava (Anna was Greek) every week.

Those who had been with the Department for years noticed the change and asked me with dark humor "What drugs are you giving her?" All I was giving her was the opportunity to contribute and an appreciation for her contributions. It was simple and miraculous.

Each chapter that addresses one of the 7 Questions includes a section on why the question and conversation around it is important, i.e., "Why it matters?" But, to begin, I want to address why leadership and supervision in a broader context matters. I learned this via a powerful experience relatively early in my career.

In the early '70's I was offered the position of Deputy Commissioner of Health for the Commonwealth of Massachusetts. How I ended up there is a long story, which is not needed to make my point. I learned a ton during my two and half years there, but no lesson was more powerful than my experience with Anna.

This experienced demonstrated to me, like no other, the power of a leader's commitment to an employee's sense of productivity and contribution. No training or reading had gotten me there. I simply wanted to know what was true for Anna. Not knowing and simply accepting her being miserable became intolerable. Knowing what was true, I could develop a plan of action for our working together, even if that meant continuing to ignore her.

The 7 Questions is simply a refinement of that basic conversation. That is finding out what is now true for the employee as well as what the employee wishes was true.

It takes some courage to ask these questions of an unhappy employee. Leaders are naturally anxious that they will hear that it is their own action or inaction which is the cause. Good leaders feel responsible for whatever the condition of an employee might be. So, if anxious that it may be our fault, we often don't ask. I didn't have that fear as I had inherited Anna's condition. It made it easier to ask. But, having asked and gotten this result, I overcame any reserve that I had to find the truth.

To this day, I remain grateful to Anna for this powerful lesson. My hope is that this story has brought to mind a similar experience you may have lost sight of or has kindled your interest in having such an experience. I would urge you to dive into the following chapters on the 7 Questions to prepare for such a conversation with the employee you're most anxious about. The rewards are huge.

5. The 7 Questions

HAVING A CONVERSATION with a direct report about the employee's performance often raises anxiety for both parties and is sometimes avoided for that reason.

For the employee, the reasons for discomfort likely come from their experience with annual evaluations or reviews in the past. That is, those evaluations may have been more about "What I didn't do right?" than what went well. Or, it may be that the employee is not feeling good about their performance at this point and doesn't really wish to talk about it.

For the supervisor, some of the rationalizations used to avoid these conversations include:

- *Who am I to judge? I don't feel that great about my own performance, or I don't have an objective basis for my judgment.*
- *I don't want to hurt or dampen motivation.*
- *What will be their thoughts regarding me? What feedback will I get?*
- *I know I see the situation differently than the employee does.*
- *I don't believe in the evaluation process we are using.*

But, without such dialogue there won't be employee development or performance improvement, and the supervisor will not be fulfilling the responsibility to add value to the organization. Quite simply, these conversations need to take place.

The 7 Questions are designed to make these conversations easier; to be freeing, even uplifting to both parties. After all, in any relationship when the air is cleared and both sides have been honest, there is a sense of a new beginning and new possibilities. Employing the 7 Questions can replace any anxiety while going into the conversation with a more relaxed feeling and even laughter.

Here is a suggested dialogue for introducing these conversations and the 7 Questions tool to create comfort going in.

Set the Context

Introduce the invitation for a meeting by stating something like, *"I'd like to sit down and revisit how we both are doing in helping you optimize your success here. I've got a new tool that makes it easy for us to have that discussion and to learn how we might better work together to get you there."*

At the meeting, begin with, *"I view the supervisor-employee relationship as a partnership. We both have responsibility to make the most of it. I want to learn how I can better fulfill my responsibility as a partner. Do you have any questions or thoughts before we start?"*

"All right. What I am going to do is ask you a series of 7 Questions. Each question requires only a 'yes' or 'no' answer. Each question focuses on whether I have fulfilled one of my responsibilities to you to set you up for success. If there is more that I can do in any of the areas covered by the question, then I want you to answer with 'no' or 'somewhat.' If you do, then I am going to ask you what is missing or what else would be of benefit to you, so that I can develop a plan of action."

"For each question, if the answer is 'yes,' but you have answered the question for yourself rather than gotten the answer from me, then I want you to answer 'no.' For example, if I ask whether you are clear on what is expected of you, then you may have figured it out yourself. But you would still not be clear whether my picture of those expectations is the same as yours. So, if you don't have certainty about my expectations of you, then the answer should be 'no.' Make sense?"

"When we get to the end, we will agree on a course of action based on your answers to these questions. I will have given you my take on how

you are performing, what additional potential I see in you and we will then come to an agreement as to how we can get there. Any questions? Ready to begin?"

Then, go through each of the questions. They are as follows:

1. *Do you know what is expected of you?*

2. *Do you know what good performance looks like in your job as defined by your supervisor?*

3. *Do you get feedback on the results that you produce?*

4. *Do you have sufficient authority to carry out your responsibilities?*

5. *Do you get timely decisions in the areas where you don't have authority?*

6. *Do you have the data, resources and support needed to meet what is expected of you?*

7. *Do you get credit for the good results that you produce?*

The balance of the book discusses each of these questions in detail and gives suggestions on follow-up questions and how to get to "yes." In Chapter 7, there are further details on how to use the 7 Questions for a variety of situations.

QUESTION #1 – EXPECTATIONS

David

Early in my career, I established and managed a health project funded through President Lyndon Johnson's War on Poverty. The project entailed organizing Alaska Natives from 15 villages spread over 44,000 square miles. The intent of the effort was to empower Alaska Natives to provide for their own healthcare and to demonstrate to the Indian Health Service (a Federal agency charged with fulfilling treaty obligations in delivery of health services to Native Americans) a new model of primary care that would deliver better health outcomes.

The project was successful from its inception. About seven years into it, the board of directors issued a strong directive wanting more progress in bringing Alaska Natives into high-level management positions. My initial strategy was to create a new Director of Ambulatory Services position. I then went searching for an Alaska Native candidate with management potential.

I found David in California. Originally from our region, he had worked his way up to a supervisory position in a hospital laboratory. His technical training was as a lab technician. He had virtually no managerial or supervision training. I was counting on his intelligence, goodwill from the clinic nursing staff and my support to propel him to greatness.

David moved north. I gave him a job description, two-days of orientation (health system overview, policies, facility tour, etc.) and lots of words of encouragement. Within two weeks, he was in my office with serious doubts about his ability to succeed and those nurses were in my office complaining that not only was he not adding value, but he was making matters worse.

I counseled David to sit down with the nurses and really listen to their concerns while using his common sense to define solutions and continue to work with them to refine solutions to their problems. Well, that didn't work. He continued to frequent my office asking for help. The nurses continued to complain and the morale of everyone declined.

The effect of my counsel of David was to send him back to the lion's den with a false sense of confidence (actually I'm not sure I even accomplished that). David's strategy to overcome being uncertain was to act overly certain and to play his authority card. He didn't want to ask his staff for help or to collaborate for solutions because he was uncomfortable facing them. Feeling like an imposter, David tried to soldier on by pretending.

The cycle of David meeting with me, followed by my meeting with the nurses to plead for their patience, was repeated over and over for the next six months. At this point, David resigned and returned to California. I never heard from him again, but still fear to this day that I destroyed his self-confidence forever. What had been a real opportunity to develop a strong leader was missed because of my own lapses as a supervisor. It's a lesson that haunts me to this day.

a little dramatic

In retrospect, David was the wrong hire. He should not have been put in that ring. The elevation to being responsible for a very busy clinic with a stressed out staff of highly trained professionals was too steep a gradient. I naively assumed that David's earnest ambition, his innate intelligence, common sense and my words of encouragement would be all it would take.

At the time, I was disappointed that the clinic staff was not more patient and supportive of my strategy. Looking back, I see that they were rightly focused on delivering the best care and trying to meet the high demand for services. Inserting David into the mix only added uncertainty and delay. It was not supportive of them.

I erred in not informing David as to what he was getting into. What was a clinic manager expected to deliver? Job descriptions don't tell you that. They usually contain a few generalities, a list of activities and then the requirements to be hired. But going into a new job armed with only the job description is a recipe for failure. (I will recommend a more useful form of job description later in this chapter).

So, what did David need to know? First, I should have defined my expectations. I would have given him a clear picture of what a well-run clinic should look like and produce. Next, I should have explained to him how I would measure that the clinic was well run. I think all that David understood was that if the nurses weren't complaining, all was well.

The challenge David faced was that the majority of his staff had more training and experience. He was not senior to them for purposes of defining solutions. The road to success for him would have been to become a good facilitator of sessions in which the staff would collaborate on solutions. That way, he could have become proficient while not doing damage to the operation. I could have modeled being a good facilitator of solutions, facilitated a few for him, coached him, etc. Instead, David did not know what was expected, so he just behaved like a boss and hoped that would work.

An Example from the Other End of the Spectrum

David knew relatively nothing about the expectations I had of him. Later in my career, I experienced an organization where the opposite was in play. At one point, I was engaged by a large health insurance company in the Pacific Northwest. A relatively new vice-president who was heading a major division had asked me to help improve the clarity of direction for his team. Although he was responsible for his team, management above him was mandating goals that were creating confusion as to the priorities for the group.

During my initial meeting with the group, I asked them, "What's expected of you now? What are the priorities and how do you know?" The answer was that an astounding 125 goals had been assigned to them. I then asked the group, "Well, when you come to work, how do you decide what to go to work on?" They responded, "Well, we just wait to hear about the goal for the day because at some point in the hallway or at the coffee pot, an existing goal will be presented as an emergency or a new goal will be delivered."

In short, there were so many goals that they had become meaningless. Instead, the lack of priorities and overwhelm was debilitating. In the end, the group had so many expectations given to them that they had no clear direction.

Why This Matters

Both David and the insurance team were not clear on what to produce, what the priorities were or how they were going to be evaluated. Lack of clear expectations causes uncertainty, caution and low performance. A small percentage of employees will figure it out for themselves, but this can be perilous. They know you will be judging their performance at some point, and they want to know how you are keeping score. What results are most important to you? At best, in the absence of certainty, there will be caution in taking action. You will be asked countless questions because employees fear making a mistake. At worst, there will either be no action or actions that don't add value or potentially do harm. That's why this matters.

How to Get to "Yes" on Question 1?

Give the employee or better yet, a new applicant, a clear and thorough description of why the position exists, what it is expected to produce and how success in the position will be measured. If David had greater clarity about what he was getting into then he might have decided that he was not ready and would have prevented me from making a mistake.

Most job descriptions don't deliver this information and, thus, don't answer this question about expectations. When was the last time you looked at your job description for guidance as to what to focus on? Job descriptions are largely used to compare the value of the various jobs in your organization, i.e. what positions should be paid relative to one another. They form the basis for salary schedules, but have little utility as a tool in supervision.

The job description format I recommend includes the following:

a. Purpose of the position – Why do we have this position? What is its importance to the organization?

b. Products – What are the end results that are to be produced? Not what someone is to *do* (the focus of most job descriptions), but rather the *results* you will be looking at when evaluating performance.

   For example: For a nurse practitioner in a clinic setting, rather than being held responsible "to diagnose and treat patients," one might say, "The health condition of patients is determined and it is understood by the patients" and "The plan of action for improving health is defined." The difference here is that when we talk in terms of results or products, we can measure whether the needed end results are being produced. When we list activities, we can measure only the activity without taking into account as to whether those activities are adding value or not (see the examples below).

c. Process – A description or chart of the inputs that prompt the person in a position to go to work, the work or added value contributed by the person in that position and the outcome from that particular input. For example, input: patient complaint, work: investigation of veracity and causes of complaint, output:

response to patient followed by process or policy modification to prevent future complaints.

d. Measures of Success – What is the data that will tell both the person in the position and his/her supervisor that the job is being done well?

Had I known then what I learned from the failed experiment with David, I would have provided something along the lines of the following to provide clarity as to what is expected:

Clinic Manager

Purpose:

To assure a smoothly functioning and high quality outpatient services operation through effective supervision, process design and problem solving.

Products of Position:

- Measures of and standards for clinic performance defined and maintained.
- Clinic measures monitored and problems, i.e. below standard performance, identified.
- Solutions defined and implemented with clinic staff.
- Regular meetings held with staff to gain input about problems and ideas for improved performance.
- Processes involving diagnostic (e.g. lab, x-ray) and support services (i.e. patient travel) monitored and problems identified.
- Meetings conducted with diagnostic and support services to identify and resolve problems, improve performance.

- Staff members evaluated semi-annually and plans for improvement developed.

Process

Inputs	Value-Added	Outputs
1. Patient complaint	Determine facts. Determine causes. Develop plan of correction.	New policy, procedure or direction to staff to avoid future similar complaints.
2. Staff complaint	Determine facts. Determine causes. Develop plan of correction.	New policy, procedure or direction to staff to avoid future similar complaints
3. Below standard statistics on quality or efficiency	Determine if cause is an unusual circumstance or a system problem. Work with team to design change in process as needed.	Process improvements implemented as needed
4. Employee resignation or termination	Initiate hiring requests to HR. Screen applicants. Conduct interviews of finalists and make hiring decision. Orient new hire.	Vacancies filled

Measures of Success

- # of patient complaints
- Employee turnover
- # of patients seen
- Audit results on conformance with treatment protocols

Had I provided all of this, one of the two alternatives to the unhappy outcome with David may have resulted in as follows: **1)** he may not have taken the job knowing what was expected, or **2)** he and I would have had a much better dialogue about his coaching needs, with effective coaching that might have been delivered by me to get him to success.

Was I to have asked the question, "Do you know or have I made clear what is expected of you?" David's honest answer would have either been "no" or "do a good job." I would have discovered that my failure was the cause of the problem. Instead of asking the question and then bringing him out of confusion, I treated the problem with continuing efforts to build an attitude of confidence versus confidence built on developed skills and certainty.

During the first 90 days on the job or on a new assignment within an existing job, check back on whether the answer to the question is still "yes." After some time on the job, the employee may very well have clarifying questions or his/her own ideas about the expectations both of which would be important to discuss. Or, like the insurance group that was overwhelmed by 125 goals, you may have sent signals about expectations or priorities that are very different from the expectations you laid out at the beginning. Doing so can create confusion about expectations or what to do first. And, again, uncertainty leads to timidity or inaction and thus lowers performance, which wouldn't have been the case with clarity.

Should you get a "no" response, here are some additional areas you may wish to probe in your dialogue in order to come up with an action plan to get to "yes":

- *Did the strategic plan or other direction bring up any questions for you regarding what is expected?*
- *Either through my actions or decisions of the management team has any confusion been created about what is expected of you or of priorities?*
- *Is there any confusion about authorities that impact the clarity of expectations?*
- *Are expectations of other departments or managers creating conflicts in the expectations or priorities of your department?*

- *Are there instances where responsibility for a result is seen as being shared with others that is creating uncertainty?*
- *Are there any policies that are creating uncertainty about expectations?*

In the Appendix are some samples for each of the four sections of a solid job description. Use these to develop the tools needed to help your staff get to a "Yes" on Question 1.

Question #2 – Good Performance

JoAnn

I hired JoAnn as an Office Manager/Consultant practically fresh off the plane. She was highly educated, wicked smart and brought several years of experience from a Chicago-based consulting firm. I considered myself lucky to have her. I thought she wouldn't need much training. I could just keep truckin' on trying to develop my consulting business, and she would cover my back on all the administrative things.

A few months into the job, I overheard her handling a phone call from a client. Her manner was abrupt and communicated disinterestedly. I had visions of what that client must be thinking about her and my business.

When JoAnn finished the call, I remarked that I wasn't happy with how she handled that call. In disbelief, she asked why. I responded with, "Well, what I want clients or prospects to experience when they talk with us is a sincere interest in them and why they are calling. I want them to get our willingness to take as long as necessary to understand why they called and to get them what they need. Instead, what I thought that client experienced was 'we aren't interested in you or your problem.' And, that is not satisfactory."

Well, JoAnn was miffed and came back with, "Well, I didn't know that. Furthermore, my boss in Chicago considered time on the phone to be wasted because it wasn't billable. He was constantly harping on me to get off the phone."

It took awhile for us to work this out. Why? JoAnn rightly objected that my standard had not been made known to her when she started. She felt that she had been set up to make a mistake, to disappoint me and to be made wrong. This could have been prevented. She was right.

By the way, this employment arrangement didn't last long either. We didn't get off on a good footing and we never quite recovered from it.

Lesson learned? Don't assume that because someone has performed a given duty for someone else that they will do the job the way you want it done.

Why this Matters

When it comes time to talk about or evaluate performance, if the supervisor employs a set of standards that have not been made known to the employee then this can easily create a conflict. Instead of intentionally setting up the employee to succeed, the supervisor unintentionally sets the employee up to lose on some level because he or she didn't know what the goal was. That is, the employee has been set up to fail. Providing clarity on standards at the very beginning gives the employee the greatest chance of meeting those standards early on.

How to Get to "Yes"

1. Recognize that you have your own standards for how the responsibilities given to your employees should be performed. Those standards may be hidden or you may not be able to articulate them, but they are there. With each new hire or each new responsibility you assign, take the time to get a clear picture in your own mind as to what an ideal handling of that responsibility would look like. Then, share it.

   Encourage dialogue about it because the employee may have a viewpoint as to what leads to good outcomes that may not be familiar to you. If so, be open to amending your own standards.

To help define your standards, look back on those who have been in the position before, describe the performance of a peak performer and then define the performance of someone whose performance didn't meet your standards. Being clear on these two points will enable you to give clarity to the new employee as to what you key off of in evaluating their performance. What matters to you? Is it timeliness? Being error free? Is it attitude? Being a self-starter? How about productivity? Being a team player?

Understand and communicate the small things that are important to you. In the example with JoAnne, it was not that she failed to answer the calls; it was *how* she handled them. Her view is that those subtleties were not a big deal, but to me personally, they were important.

The dialogue might include comments like these:

- *"What's particularly important to me is that ...."*
- *"Basic standards are to achieve...................."*
- *"Achieving .... would be a real bonus."*
- *"The errors or omissions that particularly concern me are......................."*
- *"What I have found with others is that .... is particularly challenging"*
- *"I have noticed in that past that................... This is the area in which I think we don't have the same picture as to what is important."*

2. Deliver or communicate your expectations up front. Supervisors don't do this because they think it will be received as an insult to the employee's intelligence or that they will be seen as negatively evaluating the employee before they ever start (e.g., you can't do this unless I make it clear how I want it done). Rather, it is felt one should assume the best and give the employee a chance to

succeed on their own. But, the truth is that despite the fact that they may have performed a given responsibility for years, the employee does not know how you want it done.

To get over being squeamish about this discussion, explain that you aren't going through your standards because you think the employee does not know what to do, but because you want certainty as to what's important to you in evaluating their performance and that you believe it is your responsibility to be clear on this. Consider sharing that not doing this in the past has been a problem for you. You want to communicate your standards clearly, so as to optimize the odds that the new employee will be judged as exemplary and have a positive experience working with you from the get-go.

QUESTION #3 – FEEDBACK

<hr>

Evelyn

Evelyn had been my executive secretary for years. I couldn't have asked for a more loyal and committed source of support. I could depend on her all the time for any task at any moment. In truth, I was spoiled rotten.

Over time as I saw her commitment to our success grow, I began to see some troubling signs. What I observed is commonly referred to as the "queen bee syndrome."

The secretary to the CEO possesses considerable informal power. That person sees and hears virtually every communication. That position is like the nerve center for the organization. The executive secretary becomes a confidant, e.g., the first person the CEO looks to for venting frustration. They often know the boss better than anyone in the organization. The other employees' key off what that person says and does as a way of gauging where the boss might be coming from on any given day.

Well, a "queen bee" uses that informal power to get what she wants from others. Though having no formal authority over others, they begin getting others to do work "for the boss." Given that they have the ear of the boss, no one questions this, but over time they come to resent it.

This was the case with Evelyn. The other secretaries in the executive suite began grumbling. They didn't like her attitude and didn't like her tone of voice when "asking" for help. Through the doorway, I could see this in their faces and their body language was screaming at me. I had a bit of a revolt in the making.

Because Evelyn was always going above and beyond in delivering what I needed, I didn't confront her about this. But, it got worse. So, when it came time for her annual evaluation, I delivered the message that I wasn't happy with how she interacted with the other staff and that it was having a negative impact upon morale.

Evelyn responded, rather incensed, "How long have you been concerned about this?" I replied, "Oh, about eight months." Now she really was upset, "You mean you have been disappointed in me all that time and never communicated it? Had I known I would have had a shot at correcting this before it became a problem. And, besides, those women need better supervision because they aren't delivering for this team and they should be called on it. I am doing all the work around here."

Well, she was right on all fronts. Indeed, she was performing at a level far above the others. Our relationship deteriorated for a considerable time. The work still got done, but there was a chill in the air. We weren't having fun. Ultimately, we weathered it. I fell on my sword and apologized for not being more honest with her, earlier. She deserved that from me.

In the One Minute Manager, Ken Blanchard talks about the importance of delivering One Minute Praisings and One Minute Reprimands as soon as possible after the results are detected. The problem with Evelyn arose because I didn't do that.

Why This Matters

No doubt my failing caused a good deal of unhappiness, lowered motivation and a decline in performance with Evelyn. All of this could have been avoidable. That's why this matters.

Productive working relationships are both open and honest. Withholding feedback or delivering feedback late is in some ways a betrayal. The employee trusts that you are being open, honest and are committed to their success at the company. But then, you spring on them feedback at their annual evaluation that should have been shared with them months ago. Now, the trust is eroded.

I am not a great fan of the annual evaluation process as normally practiced because it is not frequent enough. Painted as objective, e.g., your score is a 4 on a 1-5 scale, when in reality it is subjective. The evaluation is often tied to compensation changes, which raises anxiety and takes the focus off performance improvement. The employee is waiting to hear about changes in compensation rather than working with you on a plan to improve performance.

I believe there should be regular conversations around the 7 Questions, conducted no less than semi-annually. This would be an improvement on the usual annual evaluation.

Going a step further, I have now made it my own practice to give feedback on virtually every work product or client handling by my staff. I am specific on whether it met my standard or exceeded it and what it is that I particularly liked about it. If I feel it could have been done better then I communicate that as well.

Competence and performance is raised rather like going up a flight of stairs. You take a step, you steady yourself and then you take the next step. Each step represents a new skill or a first-time independent action by the employee. In this metaphor, the supervisor encourages the employee to take the next step and then provides feedback on how it went along with any needed coaching in order to steady the risk taker on that new step.

As an example, I have developed a number of office managers over the years. One of their responsibilities is to manage cash flow. When starting out, they have no clue as to what is important to pay now, how much to hold in reserve, etc. Every two weeks we go through the exercise of looking at cash on hand, receivables due and payables and decide how to manage the cash. Then, I move to having the office manager prepare a set of recommendations based on how we have managed the cash in the past (first step). Ultimately, when they get to the top of the stairs, I am simply told what I am going to be paid this time around. I overstate this a bit, but you get the idea. Having invested the time early on, my time is now freed up forever more. It is the feedback on the recommendations that built confidence to be able to act independently. While armed with that confidence, several office managers have gone on to start their own companies, which I consider a personal success.

It has consistently been both my experience and the experience of those I have taught, that when you provide constructive criticism or feedback, employees are relieved. Employees can sense if you aren't thrilled with them and they have already made the assumption that you judge them more harshly than you actually do. When the feedback is provided, even if critical, they are relieved as the unknown is now known, and what is known is almost always more positive than what they feared.

On another note, nobody really wants to work for someone with low standards. They may criticize you for being demanding, but if you are demanding and give them positive feedback, they know they have earned something valuable that will serve them well throughout their career.

How to Get to "Yes"

Consider adopting these habits:

1. Examine each work product of your direct reports. What I mean by work product is each work completion; a report, a new policy, revised process, marketing campaign, etc. Does that work product warrant feedback? Is it worthy of praise? Can you identify where it could have been improved? If yes, make note of it.

2. Deliver that feedback at the earliest convenience. In this day and age, you are often copied on emails with work products attached. Simply reply and provide the feedback. Invite the person to meet with you if they have questions. Quick. Easy. Immediate. Doesn't require a meeting or a phone call.

3. At least twice a year, have a formal sit down to provide general feedback. Go over the 7 Questions and identify areas to monitor for improved performance. At that time, make commitments on what steps you will make to improving performance, e.g., coaching, investment in training, assigning a mentor and continuing regular feedback on work products.

4. If you do get a "yes" to this question, understand that there may be reluctance to give you a "no" when that is the truth. So, I would suggest probing a bit on this with some follow up questions:

   - *Would you appreciate feedback more often?*
   - *Could my feedback be more precise to be actionable by you? Can you give me an instance in which I was not precise?*
   - *Are there areas of your performance that you are uncertain about, like whether you are meeting standards?*

When asking an employee to answer Question #3, you are asking them if they understand whether they are doing a good job <u>on an ongoing basis</u>, not if they were clear on how you evaluated their performance 6-12 months ago. If the employee does not hear any feedback for months, doubt creeps into their minds as to whether you remain satisfied with their work. Employees are reading your body language and tone of voice all the time to get a handle on this. Instead of having them guess, communicate.

Question #4 – Authority

Jackie

Jackie had worked her way up in the group practice for years while demonstrating her loyalty to the owners and commitment to hard work. When personnel problems kept mounting, the owners decided to elevate Jackie to "manager." She now had taken on the responsibility for an office where backstabbing was the regular diet. What the owners failed to do was define and communicate to the staff the authority for her new responsibilities. Let me explain.

After months of frustration for the owners and Jackie alike, I was brought in to help rectify the situation. I quickly assessed that Jackie was the "manager" in name only. She had no real authority to manage. So, I started at the top, "Who is in charge?" The owners responded that they both were and that all decisions were made by consensus of the two owners. In other words, they saw themselves as the authority on decisions. But, it was clear that the two never met to hear and resolve issues, and that they had very different standards. In reality, the issues were not resolved. Not only had they retained the authority that Jackie needed to succeed, but their actions and decisions formed no basis for Jackie to be consistent in her supervision.

Employees would go around Jackie to whichever owner they thought would be receptive and then that owner, without consulting the partner, would issue a decision. Decisions were inconsistent. In effect, there were no policies. The practice moved from crisis to crisis. With each decision by the owners, Jackie's effectiveness as "manager" was further undermined.

Jackie's need for authority was not met. Policies that she could implement were not established. The owners, who were besieged by employees who were trying to work the non-system for their own ends, blamed Jackie for the chaos. Jackie was in tears. Her health was failing. We had a real crisis here.

I sat the two owners and Jackie down and got an agreement on a simple set of policies that Jackie would have the authority to enforce. I got a pledge from the owners that they would announce both the policies and Jackie's new authority at an all staff meeting. I implored the owners to resist meeting with employees to hear their grievances and to insist that employees work through Jackie. I also got a commitment that the owners would meet with Jackie regularly to assess the situation and solve problems together.

Well, too little too late. Jackie had already been undermined to the point that it couldn't be rehabilitated.

What Happened Here and Why This Matters?

The owners wanted to have nothing to do with the day-to-day management. Their first commitment was to their patients. Managing the practice was a bother. They had no time for Jackie, but always seemed to have time for the disgruntled employees who would grab them when Jackie was gone. On top of all this, Jackie was going to graduate school. In short, Jackie was given responsibility to create a problem-free office that delivered great service to patients, but given no authority to make it happen. The owners wanted the problems to go away, but did not understand that without supporting Jackie and giving her authority, that would never happen.

Lacking faith and trust in her, they simply made her a buffer between the owners and the problems they didn't want to solve. So, the problems didn't get solved and Jackie's self-esteem continued to erode. This was really cruel.

When I confronted the owners with my view of the situation, they were repentant. They wanted Jackie to succeed. They just didn't know how to make it happen. They did not understand how their actions to please all the employees were undermining her authority. They were just trying to meet the needs of aggrieved employees the same way they treated patients in crisis. The gap between the expectations of Jackie and their authority created an impossible mission for her to succeed in.

I have seen this at all levels. I worked with a CEO of a holding company in a scenario in which the board was holding him accountable for subsidiary performance, but the subsidiary CEO's worked for subsidiary boards. After a few years of this, the CEO finally stood up and said, "You can't hold me accountable for their performance because I have no authority over them."

Having sufficient authority is not just a function of what is defined in a job description or policy, but also in the leadership practice that affects that position. If the judgment of a manager is always being second-guessed or reversed and there is freedom for subordinates to go around the supervisor, then the supervisor doesn't have real authority to get the needed results.

Another common problem surrounds the authority to hire. That is, if I can't pick and/or terminate the members of a team that are expected to perform at a certain level, then it is not fair to hold me accountable when the team doesn't meet that level of performance.

When lacking sufficient authority, one tends to avoid the responsibility rather than rise up to meet it. Rising up can be challenging. It brings up the common fear of failure. It's easier to justify not rising up because you don't have any real authority. Jackie, bless her heart, beat herself up instead. She was given an impossible mission and should have protested that from the beginning. However, she was loyal and grateful to the owners for supporting her start in the company and continuing her education.

How to Get to "Yes"

1. Just ask Question 4 and insist on an honest answer. Other ways to ask the question or to get into dialogue about this might be:

- "Am I expecting something from you that you can't deliver?"
- "Are my own actions undermining your ability to get those results?"
- "What specific authority do you need from me to be able to accomplish what I am expecting?"

2. If you want others to fulfill the responsibilities you have given them, then you have to give them the authority and support them in exercising it. That means, being patient when initial mistakes are made.

   To stabilize the employee on that next step of the stairway, you will need to let go. Resist the tendency to review draft products or decisions *once they are fully hatted with the new authority*. If you don't, then you will continue to be making those decisions into the future. Be very explicit that you don't want to review the decision or product before it is implemented. It is common for employees to want to hedge their bets indefinitely by having you review draft products. But, your goal should be to get them operating completely independently as I did with my office managers and managing cash flow.

   If it turns out after letting go that the results are not optimal, then learning will happen and there will be future improvement (this assumes that you can tolerate the cost of a mistake, i.e., letting go of brain surgery may not be advisable). In the short run, you may choose to provide coaching as I described with new office managers, but your goal should be to take the training wheels off as soon as possible.

3. With a new manager or one that you don't have confidence in, rather than pull back the authority, try increasing the level of coaching. Make it clear what decisions you want them to confer with you on. Then, make time for that to happen. Coach to the ability to exercise authority independently as soon as possible. Having to confer with you on decisions means that someone is

waiting for a decision, progress may be slowed and subordinates of your employee may be losing confidence in that supervisor.

Which Leads Me to Question #5

QUESTION #5 – TIMELY DECISIONS

ONE OF THE things Jackie tried to do to resolve her situation at the group practice was implement a set of personnel policies. She indicated that she had been trying to establish personnel policies for some time, but couldn't get the attention of the owners. One of the agreements I got the owners to make early on was to empower Jackie by working with her to establish a set of policies that could be agreed upon.

Jackie had no previous experience with drafting policies, but she had done her research and delivered a set of draft policies to the owners for their approval. Jackie waited six months for a decision. She could not even get a meeting to discuss what she had proposed. Yet, the owners' expectations that she maintain a problem-free work environment remained in place. This was an unfair expectation under such circumstances, and prevented Jackie from achieving her potential.

In essence, they not only failed to provide Jackie with the authority to establish policy (Question #4), but they wouldn't make a decision themselves on policy either.

You may be asking, "How could this be? How could you give someone responsibility, but then not provide either the authority to make decisions, or at the very least, the decisions themselves?" It happens all the time. A governing board might do this to a CEO or a holding company to a subsidiary CEO or an owner to an office manager, which was the case with Jackie.

Why This Matters

Let's look at how this impacts performance. Suppose a supervisor expects the office manager to be sure that their vendors are happy and that there is no interest expense due to late payments to vendors. Well, if the supervisor sits on the cash flow report and set of recommendations on the use of cash, then the office manager can't achieve that performance standard. The delay in decision-making by the supervisor would be the cause of the delay in paying the bills and the incurring interest expense. The supervisor is holding the employee to an unfair standard because the standard cannot be met.

Very important to success here is defining "timely" in Question 5. Who defines the standard for "timely?" The answer is, "The person you are supervising." That person needs the decision when they need it. You may not understand their urgency, but they are the one you are holding accountable for the performance standard. Having a conversation on what "timely" looks like will inform you as to the impact of delays. Knowing that, you can develop a plan to either deliver decisions when needed or expand the authority of your subordinate to make decisions on his or her own.

How to Get to "Yes"

"Yes" would mean that the timing of your decision-making is not slowing performance. With Question 5, you are asking if more responsive decision-making would improve subordinate performance.

Couch the question in terms, so that the employee does not feel like they are accusing you of being indecisive or slow. Rather, you are simply inquiring as to what impact the current practice of decision-making (could be by you, could be by your boss or could be by the board of directors) is having on performance.

Some suggested practices to help get to "yes" are as follows:

1. Regularly monitor what decisions are needed from you.

2. When asked to make a decision, inquire as to when it is needed. After you agree upon when the decision will be made, then just honor that commitment.

3. Recognize as early as possible that you don't have sufficient information to make the needed decision and be specific in your request for additional information.

4. If you find subordinates bringing you decisions that they should be making themselves, ask them, "Have my previous leadership actions trained you to bring these decisions to me rather than make them yourself?" If yes, then communicate that you believe the employee is ready to make the decisions on his/her own and that not doing so is delaying progress and their own development. Encourage the employee that making a mistake is OK and that the worst that can happen is you both learn from it.

For the employee, giving a "no" answer is a high risk. You will need to work hard to get the employee comfortable being truthful here. Be cautious to not get defensive. Also, understand that you may feel as if a decision was made, but the communication was such that it wasn't clear to the employee. Some follow-on questions might include:

- *Would more rapid decisions have made a difference? Which decisions?*
- *How did the delay waiting for a decision impact you?*
- *Were the decisions untimely or incomplete/unclear? Which decisions?*

Question 5 can be a sticky one when the employee feels a "no" answer is a rebuke to the supervisor asking the question. Working toward a "yes," however, can be laid out in some simple steps that allow an employee to state what he or she needs in a non-confrontational manner.

The goal should be for the employee to deploy all of their existing skills and be unimpeded in contributing to the productivity and quality of the organization. Waiting for decisions can be a major barrier to that end, but is often the most challenging of the questions to solicit an honest answer to. Using the follow-on questions that I have suggested above is a means to overcome timidity in being honest.

Matt

Matt was hired as the Director of Information Technology for a rapidly growing non-profit company with about 225 employees and over 25 programs. Initially, despite a heavy backlog and a host of discouraged users, the job was relatively simple. It was basic PC support; software updates, user education, updating machines and maintaining a relatively simple server system. Early on, any help was much appreciated by users. Matt was happy. Having waited so long for support to come along, users were willing to wait a bit longer to get real help. When the help arrived, Matt got accolades. Because of the backlog, he needed to clone himself to meet the demand, but he knew once he had done that, it would be clear sailing. He got approval for a new hire, made his clone and then life was good.

But, the organization continued to grow geometrically both in size and complexity. First, there was implementing a complex billing system that was to be integrated across numerous programs. Then, there was the need to purchase, install and configure a phone system that was fully integrated with other systems. Looming on the horizon was the mandate for a new electronic medical record system to be implemented across several programs. The new record system needed substantial customization and would require the reliance on outside vendors to manage it. All of this made Matt anxious. The pressures were becoming intense, indeed.

What initially was a satisfying job had become a highly frustrating one. Matt was a man of high standards and integrity. He stood behind his systems. He was at the point where he thought he did not have the personal bandwidth to maintain today's systems and prepare the organization for the future. Instead of being excited about the future and feeling appreciated, Matt felt demoralized. He foresaw his personal standards would be at risk. He tried to caution management about the pace of change and lack of resources, but was not successful. His previous success and confidence in him resulted in his cautions falling on deaf ears.

Matt's contributions at management team meetings shifted from laying out what would be possible to protecting himself and his troops by limiting expectations of his department. His commitment to the purpose of the organization never wavered, but his production suffered. He began to complain about the lack of incentives for himself and his employees. "I can push them harder, but what's in it for them?"

Matt was caught in a dilemma. It appeared to him that his choices were either: **1)** lower standards for himself and his staff to execute quick, but potentially unstable fixes, or **2)** continue to push both himself and his staff for a level of production he considered to be unfair. Like all dilemmas, Matt didn't like either of the choices. He did not want himself associated with substandard work and he didn't want to be unfair in his expectations of his staff, especially when he didn't have authority to reward them for going beyond the normal call of duty.

Why This Matters

The dilemma faced by Matt is common. It is found amongst the highly competent and committed. Superiors come to rely on such individuals to deliver results. And, thus the expectations continue to rise. Not wanting to let superiors or the organization down, the Matts of the world press on until they get to the point where their motivation and production deteriorates.

Matt, if asked, would have likely suggested some combination of the following to solve his dilemma:

- Secure consulting help for evaluation and/or installation of new systems.
- Temporary authority to offer rewards to employees putting in extra time.
- Additional staffing.
- Some delay in the implementation of new systems.

However, Matt would not have easily welcomed reliance on outside resources (he was a 'do-it-myself to get it right' kind of guy and had been burned by outside resources before) or a delay in the new systems (he was committed to I.T. delivering as much as he was to organizational performance).

Matt should have never been put in the position of having to decide between unacceptable alternatives. He was in that position because Question #6 had not been asked and addressed soon enough.

The intent of Question #6 is to enable a supervisor to recognize the threat of a dilemma, like Matt's, before it is too late. "Too late," meaning there is a negative impact on motivation, morale and performance. Question #6, along with others, is intended to assess whether the "contract" (expectations vs. rewards) that you have with your employee is fair. This issue of fairness will be addressed more fully in Chapter 6.

How to Get to Yes?

It may be challenging to get an honest reply to Question 6. The Matts of the world, i.e., high achievers, don't like admitting that they can't get it done. They may reply, "I really appreciate you asking and your concern. I'm just having a bit of a bad day. I think we can get it under control here before too long." It is a matter of pride for these folks to be self-reliant and meet any challenges. So, one may need to explore a bit deeper to get to the truth and a real solution. The dialogue might go something like this:

> *Supervisor: "Matt, from listening to you at our management team meetings, it appears that you are experiencing a high workload and stress within your department. True?"*
>
> *Matt: "Yes, it has been tough lately. It seems like everything is coming all at once. There have been an unusual number of breakdowns. But, we will get through it. I appreciate your asking."*
>
> *Supervisor: "Well, it seems as if it has been going on for awhile. Do you really see it letting up?"*
>
> *Matt: "Yes, I think so. We just need to catch a break."*
>
> *Supervisor: "OK. So, tell me more about the impact upon you, your troops and your outcomes from the current situation, since it has been going on for some time?"*
>
> *Matt: "Well, I think the troops are a bit frustrated because they can't get ahead, and I am riding them hard all the time. We used to have a good time together, but now we all seem a bit testy."*
>
> *Supervisor: "Understandable, but tell me what the impact is upon you?"*
>
> *Matt: "Well, I'm just concerned that because we're moving so fast, I may be missing something. I would really like to have more time to understand and evaluate the new systems we are considering, but I don't feel right leaving all the day-to-day work to my staff because they are overloaded."*

Supervisor: "Matt, I've been in situations like yours before. It wore on me, and I know it wears on you. I appreciate you wanting to take it all on yourself, but I also want to be sure we do these evaluations right and that you are confident that the new systems are going to work for us. Shouldn't we consider some alternatives to get us through this rough patch?"

Matt: "Well, I'm not sure I would trust anyone else to do the evaluations, and bringing on new staff would just mean a further drag on me because I would have to train them up to do things right."

Supervisor: "I totally understand that, Matt, but I also don't want the price of this to be burning out you or your staff, or causing costly mistakes to be made because we are going too fast. Are there any tasks that we could trust an outside resource to handle for us? Maybe some low level investigations of the experience other users have had with these new systems that would save you some time? Maybe contract some of the more basic PC support to an outside firm?"

Matt: "I'm not sure that is going to work, but I appreciate the offer."
Supervisor: "Do I need to scale back the expectations of your department, or delay some of these implementations?"
Matt: "I know how important these new systems are to our future and besides, some of these are mandated upon us. I don't think that is a solution."

Supervisor: "OK, but I would like you to give this further thought. Can we set up a time for you and I to meet after you have considered what might be helpful to get you out of this dilemma? I believe continuing on as we are would be too great a risk."

Matt: "I'm not sure I have time for that."

Supervisor: "Matt, I need you to make time for that. This situation is potentially dangerous. I don't want to lose you or to make costly mistakes. So, make the time to put together some proposals for me to consider. Now, when can we meet on this?"

Sound familiar? What we are looking at here is that Matt is likely going home and complaining to his wife about being overloaded by the unfairness of the situation. Matt is a ticking time bomb. So, in having conversations like this with a dedicated employee, like Matt, you have to probe deeper and make it safe for the employee to receive help. Matt's instinctive reaction is to blame himself and view such a conversation as a sign of his own failure. The predictable response is to toughen up. But, that rubber band will eventually break and either Matt or his staff will likely depart.

In the dialogue above, the supervisor is seeing the truth in Matt's body language and comments at management meetings. Quite correctly, the supervisor is choosing to confront these warning signs.

Once you know the truth of what is occurring, you can develop a plan of action to correct the situation. That plan of action might include short-term adding of resources, as was the case for Matt. In the long-term, the solution for Matt would be better planning by the management team for future IT services, so that the needed resources are in place to execute projects well.

A Word of Caution: Knowing Whether You Have the Right Resources

Take one note of caution on Question #6. When it comes to deciding whether there are sufficient resources, there is another truth operating here that should make you pause. Rarely does someone, when asked, state that they have enough time or resources to do what's expected of them. After all, if they did the conclusion might be that they have a lot of spare time on their hands. Rather, a supervisor or CEO is always facing pressure at budget time to provide more resources in order to get the job done right. If a supervisor or CEO always accedes to this pressure, the company may become non-competitive due to excessive costs. Ideally, an organization should be lean and mean, which would mean that you may often hear that personnel are stretched thin. Lean and mean is good, but stretched too thin is not. How to make the call?

A Case in Point

Early in my career when running a rural health system, my organization took ownership of a small rural hospital. As I familiarized myself with the condition of the hospital as a whole and of each department, I became aware that there was a problem with delays in getting completed patient encounter forms into the patients' medical records. These records were stacking up on the desk of the medical records supervisor, waiting to be properly coded. When patients returned for follow-up visits, the records could not be located (this was some time ago when paper records were still being used), so physicians did not have access to information from previous visits, medications, etc. This was a potentially dangerous situation.

I confronted the medical records supervisor who responded with a tale of woe about being overworked. "Understood," I said, "I will get you some help." Well, I authorized another position for her department. The situation did not change. Then, another position was authorized, but no change. Finally, a third position, but no change. Each time my conversation with the supervisor was a repeat of the story about being overworked.

Ultimately, I came to the conclusion that the thing lacking was not the resources, but the organizational and supervisory skills. So, we mutually agreed to part our separate ways.

I recruited a new medical records supervisor. She came in and, in less than six months, not only had eliminated the backlog, but implemented an entirely new record system and had done so without filling some vacancies in her department. At that point, she was in my office complaining about being bored.

The moral of the story is that a "no" answer to Question #6 should signal the need for an evaluation of the quality of supervision and work processes to determine the root cause of the backlog. It should signal an automatic call for adding resources.

How to Get to the Truth

Areas of investigation to determine the root cause might include the following:

- How well are employees under the supervisor being oriented, trained and utilized?
- Are the existing processes within the department undermining the ability of employees to be productive?
- How does to ratio of employees to output compare with peers (if such data is available)?

Should you get a "no" answer to Question #6 regarding resources, then you need to continue the dialogue to get clarity here. Some follow-on questions might be as follows:

- *Is it a particular expertise that is lacking?*
- *Is this the result of someone in the group not meeting standards?*
- *Is the workload evenly balanced across your team?*
- *What are the indicators that the workload is unrealistic?*
- *Are there ways in which processes or methods could be streamlined, so that more could be accomplished with the resources we have?*
- *What data is missing and how would it be used?*
- *What was the impact of the lack of support?*
- *What are the instances in which support was lacking?*
- *What would the needed support have looked like?*
- *Would the solution involve more resources or more recognition and credit for better results?*
- *What would a solution look like to you?*

Once the root causes have been determined, you and the supervisor can develop a plan of action to correct the situation. The plan of action might include short-term adding of resources as was the case for Matt and his IT department. It may also be improving the ability of the supervisor to organize, streamline processes and gain better productivity from his/her employees.

QUESTION #7 – CREDIT

Dave

Dave had worked for Interior Air for nearly 15 years. Although not a member of the family that owned the business, Dave felt part of the family. He had joined the second generation of family owners and other friends as part of that transition. The company had grown rapidly and had been consistently successful. Dave was an integral part of the meteoric rise of the company and felt that his contributions were appreciated.

Initially, Dave was responsible for accounting and oversaw most administrative functions. Having stabilized those operations, he took on the challenge of building the information technology systems that would give Interior an advantage over its competitors. He had personally written the code for a package tracking system that performed much like the tracking system of FedEx. However, none of Interior's competitors had anything like this system. In short, Dave was highly responsible and met every challenge given to him.

As the organization grew, Dave was often the only one with the courage to speak the truth about problems in management's team meetings. This should have been invaluable, but Interior was obsessed with growth and didn't want to hear about or address these problems. Furthermore, the management team could not see the potential of taking advantage of Dave's package tracking system to achieve competitive advantage. Leadership was pilot-centric. Slowly, but surely, Dave was becoming dispirited while his contributions to discussion of strategy and priorities were being marginalized. He no longer felt the appreciation and satisfaction he once did, although no one recognized his waning enthusiasm.

At about the same time, it became apparent that the CEO was spread too thin. A family member, he was heading the company when Dave first joined, but then left the company for a number of years. He returned to the position to find a very different company from the one he had left. Larger, more complex, more regulated.

He was trying to juggle strategizing and executing growth initiatives, overseeing operations, performing check rides on pilots and filling in when pilots were out ill or on vacation. It was not doable. Unless this got fixed, the rapid growth of Interior would stall out. Either more management resources or a dramatic change in delegation by the CEO were going to be needed to solve the problem.

I suggested to the CEO that we approach Dave about assuming more management responsibilities and finding someone to take over his I.T. duties. I was given a green light to approach Dave with the idea. The conversation set me back and taught me a valuable lesson.

To summarize Dave's response, it went something like this:

"Why would I want to bail him out? If he didn't want to be CEO, he shouldn't have taken the job. I have enough pressures already. There's nothing in it for me to take on those pressures."

There were two forces at play here. On the one hand, there was resentment that the CEO was not meeting the needs of the organization for leadership and decision-making. On the other hand, Dave wasn't getting enough credit for what he was contributing. So, he couldn't justify committing to contributing more. Had Dave gotten his due credit for his contributions in the past, I sense this conversation might have gone differently.

Why This Matters

Dave, like Matt in the previous chapter, was a peak performer. Peak performers are often saddled with the tough challenges others aren't willing to take on. Over time, they feel taken advantage of. They likely have a tough time admitting to that, but may do so when asked directly if they have received sufficient credit for past results.

Again using the rubber band analogy, employees like Dave and Matt can be stretched very thin, so that the band can snap quickly and unexpectedly. Once it does, it is very difficult to repair.

Therefore, Question 7 matters because it can uncover a hidden risk factor. A risk that will not surface unless you have a very acute sense for the warning signs, e.g. less participation in meetings, rolling the eyes in management team meetings, less humor and withdrawal. Again, this question when presented properly can unearth what is difficult to get at.

How to Get to "Yes"

What influences whether or not a subordinate will answer "yes?" Here are some factors to investigate as you dialogue with them:

- *Have their contributions been acknowledged and appreciated?*
- *Given how they have performed relative to their peers, do they feel as if they have been taken advantage of?*
- *Do they see you holding others accountable for performing to the same extent?*
- *Has public recognition in the form of compensation, promotions etc. been fair in relation to others?*

In our story, Dave had reached the end of the line. He was no longer willing to extend himself to aid the CEO or the company because he thought he was being taken advantage of.

You might begin the conversation on this question by admitting that you don't always take the time to appreciate the efforts of those contributing to making you and the company successful. Express that there have been times when you have felt taken advantage of and you don't want others to experience that, which is why this question is important to you. That way, you begin by accusing yourself rather than leaving it to the employee to accuse you of being unfair. The employee is only affirming what you already know about yourself. This will work only if true or sincere.

Such an opening can create an entry point for honest dialogue. It is our nature to want to be appreciated and feel as if we are helping something or someone we believe in. Not feeling appreciated impacts motivation and, in turn, performance. The ability to get to "yes" is important for creating job satisfaction amongst you and your employee.

The rest of the conversation with Dave might have gone like this:

Supervisor: Dave, I'm particularly interested in whether you feel as if you have been given due credit for the results that you have produced. Much went on before I came back to the company. I know you contributed a great deal to our success. So, do you feel as if you were given due credit for those results?

Dave: It's been all right. Lots of us contributed. It was a team effort.
Supervisor: OK. I appreciate that, but feeling as if you got credit for results is a personal thing. What's your own calculation in regard to this question? Has the company been fair to you?

Dave: Well, not really.

Supervisor: OK. Well what should have happened either on my watch or before I came back?

Dave: To be truthful, I felt that I should have been given a bigger raise when I took on overseeing all administrative functions. Not getting that was one reason why I wanted to give it up.

Supervisor: I can see that. What about since you have been oversee-ing I.T.? I know you have made great strides there.

Dave: Well, I see my developing the package tracking software as having saved us a bunch of money and given us a huge competitive advantage. I thought I should have been considered for issuance of some company stock for that contribution.

Supervisor: All right. I really appreciate you being honest with me. I know it was difficult. I need to give this some consideration. My commitment to you is that we come to an agreement that seems fair to both of us. Let me give this some thought and get back to you.

For Dave, such a conversation might have been too little, too late. Dave had become a "won't do" employee in regards to taking on additional responsibilities. He was doing well on what was expected of him now. The "won't do" was associated with considerations about contributing more. His viewpoint might change over time if he were to feel more appreciated. But for now, with his sense of fairness having been violated, it was a very tough sell.

As with some of the previous questions, a truthful answer may be hard to secure. The employee may think that humility is the best course here. Some additional questions to get dialogue going on this might be as follows:

- *"Do you feel as if your efforts are appreciated?"*
- *"Am I or others taking credit where credit should be given to you?"*
- *"Looking at your contributions relative to your peers and to the credit they have received, have we been fair with you?"*
- *"Is there anything that would increase your motivation to contribute here?"*

Getting to a "yes" on this question is not just about "attaboys." That is, credit may mean more than recognition. It may even involve compensation. You may remember that fairness of compensation for those going over and above the call of duty was also an issue for Matt and his I.T. staff. The impact of calculations about fairness upon answers to all the Questions will be addressed in more detail in the next chapter.

6. THE UNDERLYING PRINCIPLE OF FAIRNESS

Fair: def. – being in accordance with relative merit or significance.
Exchange: def. – to give in return for something received.

THE QUALITY OF human relationships is governed by several key factors, among them being honest, the ability to understand one another, level of agreement and fairness of exchange. Fairness is the key to understanding the condition of and to debugging the employer-employee relationship.

Think of your own marriage or those that you have observed. What are the root causes of most arguments? I would offer that they lie in fairness of exchange, i.e., whether or not the parties are doing their "fair share;" be it chores, earning money, raising children or even sex. When one party feels that the exchange is no longer fair, the disagreements begin.

My partner, Doug, and I have had a successful business partnership for over 25 years. Have we had differences? Of course, but we are both human and we are committed to being fair to one another. When the relative contribution to the business has shifted, our partnership agreement has had to change. We have made such adjustments numerous times over the years. Once the adjustments are made, we can turn our attention to improving our products, designing new ones and collaborating in meeting client needs. We don't harbor resentments. We don't avoid one another. Whenever we have let an unfair exchange go on too long, we stopped communicating, stopped collaborating and, ultimately, stopped producing as a partnership. Instead, we continued on in our own little world with our clients while harboring unexpressed resentment.

There is no magic formula for determining fairness. Each individual has their own consideration on the value they are providing relative to the value being contributed by the other party. The only way to keep the relationship healthy and productive is to maintain regular dialogue on whether it still feels fair. If either party feels it is not, then you need to communicate towards a solution that works for both parties. It is no easy task because it is difficult to appreciate someone else's point of view on the value of your work versus theirs.

Let's look at the 7 Questions and how they pertain to exchange:

1. *Do you know what is expected of you?*

2. *Do you know what good performance looks like in your job as defined by your supervisor?*

3. *Do you get feedback on the results that you produce?*

4. *Do you have sufficient authority to carry out your responsibilities?*

5. *Do you have the data, resources and support needed to meet what is expected of you?*

6. *Do you get timely decisions in the areas where you don't have authority?*

7. *Do you get credit for the good results that you produce?*

Questions #1-3 are designed to enable the employee to deliver the results needed. It is simply not fair to expect certain results without making it clear as to what those results should be. Doing so would likely prompt the response, "How can you make me wrong for not doing what I didn't know I was supposed to be doing in the first place?" This is why Questions #1 & 2 are so important.

It is also not fair to have the employee wondering whether they have met your standards or not. If you do not provide that feedback and then wait until the annual evaluation, as I did with Evelyn (see Ch. 3), you will likely get an irritated response along the lines of, "Why didn't you tell me sooner, so I could have corrected this?" This is why Question #3 is vital.

Not taking action to assure a "yes" answer to these questions will lead to a fundamental sense of unfairness. You may be saying that you see the relationship as a partnership to get to the employee's full potential, but you are not meeting your end of the bargain. The employee can't deliver what you expect because you haven't provided what is needed to make that happen. Over time, resentment will build, communication will break down, production will not be acceptable and the relationship will be under serious threat.

Questions #4, #5 & #6 verify whether the expectations are fair under the current conditions. To overstate, it would be like expecting your spouse to maintain clean carpets, but not being willing to buy a vacuum cleaner. This would be totally unfair.

Another Example

It is not fair to hold someone accountable for the performance of their team when they don't have authority to hire and fire that team. It is not fair to expect someone to meet a production goal when not given sufficient resources to meet that goal. It is not fair to ding me for not meeting a deadline when I didn't have the authority to make happen what was needed or didn't get timely decisions in the areas where I did not have authority.

Question #7, i.e., whether credit is given for good results is a direct measure of fairness. Credit can be recognition of various sorts, but is often measured by how results are rewarded financially. Is there fairness in the salary structure? Is there objectivity and fairness in how bonuses are rewarded? Are peak performers given due credit? Are the expectations fairly distributed or is there overreliance on peak performers who end up carrying others?

Ultimately, considerations of fairness are an evaluation of the "contract" between the organization and the employee. The employee is delivering a level of effort and performance. As supervisor, you are the administrator of that contract. Even if you cannot define the terms (e.g. salary structure, authority), you do have influence over them and you can adjust your expectations when you deem that the contract is not fair.

Are you delivering on your end of the bargain and is that bargain fair? If the employee answers "yes" to all 7 questions, then fairness exists. If not, then, as supervisor, you need to continue to work your way to "yes" through honest dialogue on what's missing and what would fill the void.

Your Own Beliefs About Fairness

Think about situations in which you have felt uncomfortable because you weren't doing your fair share. Say, someone else does all the work, but you get all the credit. Or, a friend is always reaching out to you and always picking up the tab. Do you feel that you need to even the score with them? Do you feel uncomfortable when indebted? Likely the answer is, "yes."

Now, look at how you view your employees. Do you see them as trying to take advantage of you or the organization? Are they trying to get something for nothing? Well, is that really true? How do you know that? And, why is it that you view them as having a different attitude about fairness than yourself? Do the views of management as a whole differ from your own on this question? How is the organization doing in terms of fairness with its employees?

It is true that employees and their unions often push for more compensation and more benefits. Are their requests unfair? Or, are they asking because they have not been treated fairly?

Examining the history of unions, they arose because the business barons of the day were inflicting unfair working conditions and compensation. The employees were simply trying to achieve fairness. Are they fighting for fairness now or are their demands unfair? Are they willing to be fair partners when times are tough in exchange for fairness when the organization is prospering?

Why Fairness Matters

My own experience is that when I am fair with employees, they feel an obligation to maintain their end, which is their contribution. When I initiate offering them a raise, they sense my commitment to be fair and to share success. The amount of the raise doesn't seem to be the key. It is the commitment to fairness and the expressions of appreciation of their work that has the biggest impact. My commitment to be fair and reward them for their work increases their commitment.

Alternatively, employees who sense a lack of commitment to fairness and observe benefits accruing largely to those in management will build resentment and lose commitment to the company.

Won't Do Employees and Fairness

One of the characteristics of Won't Do employees is that they have a somewhat skewed view on fairness. They sometimes lack an innate sense of fairness. Despite not actually producing, they project a high level of commitment, complain of being overworked and boast about their contributions and importance. They often are lobbying for more compensation on the grounds that they are carrying their team when in reality the opposite is true.

There are two words of caution here. Don't take a "no" response to Question #7 regarding "credit for results" at face value. Examine actual data before determining that this "no" response warrants action on your part. What data? Well, what are the actual results produced? How do those results compare with that of others doing similar work?

How does the compensation compare with those producing work at the same level? If the employee cites salaries from competitors, then secure verification of that data.

The "won't do" employee will not only mislead you in terms of hiding their non-productivity and generalizing about problems that don't exist, but also on compensation and benefits. Their sense of unfairness is based on a self-perception of higher commitment and loyalty than their peers. However, consideration of exchange should be based on production and not on behavior or attitudes.

Determine Where You Are and Strengthen the Partnership with Employees

I raise the issue of fairness only to have you look over your own views on the matter and how those views may be impacting your success in developing employees.

The 7 Questions get at whether there is fairness between supervisor/organization and the employee. They examine whether the "contract" is fair. A "no" response to any of the questions may mean that it is not.

In the previous chapters, I recommended some follow-on questions that can get you to clarity on the true condition of the "partnership" and what you need to do to strengthen it. A good follow-on question for each of the 7 Questions would focus on fairness. That is, you might get a "yes" on clear expectations, feedback, credit etc; but although they are clear, they may be perceived as unfair. Ask the question and if the employee indicates a sense of unfairness, find out why and make your own judgment on fairness. Then, propose changes to strengthen the partnership.

7. Putting the 7 Questions to Work

Think about this. Supervisors spend somewhere between 40% and 80% of their time (based on how routine the work is and how many individuals are being supervised) doing management work rather than production. Management work, by definition, does not directly contribute to the results of the organization. That is, you aren't producing a product, serving an external customer, etc. Rather, management work only adds value if it results in better performance by those who report to you. If, in a given year, the performance of your team has not improved, then the cost of your position is taking from the bottom line, not adding to it. <u>For you to add value to the company, the performance of your direct reports has to improve.</u>

Your job as supervisor is to get a genuine "yes" response to all 7 Questions. A genuine "yes" means that you have delivered what is needed rather than the employee figuring it out for him/herself. If you don't get a "yes," then you need to continue dialogue to gain clarity on what specific actions are needed by you to get to a "yes."

How You Can Add Value

The 7 Questions can serve to develop a clear and detailed plan for improved performance. It is somewhat daunting for the employee to identify what they might need from their supervisor in order to progress. The questions help identify the specifics of what is needed to get to optimum performance. The 7 Questions also serve as a pre-flight checklist to insure that we have good initial conditions for the flight ahead.

Applications of the 7 Questions

There are four applications in which the 7 Questions can play a valuable role in supervision:

1. Assessing the quality of orientation for new employees.

2. Assessing the quality of supervision.

3. Evaluating employee performance.

4. Determining the proper course of action for an underperforming employee.

1. Assessing the Quality of Orientation for New Employees

Regarding the word "orientation," I am using the term to describe the process of setting an employee up for success. It is more than a tour, introductions, going through the employee manual, etc. Orientation is about providing sufficient direction and training to where the employee can achieve success early on and with a minimum of the "learning by mistakes" method. It requires planning and patience by the supervisor and those in human relations.

Most organizations don't commit enough resources to orientation. If you have ever observed or experienced this being done well, then you know the value of the return on investment that comes from it. One organization I am familiar with puts all their new employees through a multi-week program before they begin seeing clients. The purpose is to instill the strong values and operating principles of the organization, build teaming skills and so on. By the end of the program, both the organization and the employee are clear on whether there is a fit and if success is likely to happen.

It is the supervisor that must orient the employee to the specifics of their position or new responsibility. If you have diagnosed your natural leadership style using Blanchard's Situational Leadership II® or other tools, then you likely know whether you are comfortable and skilled at being highly directive. This is what is needed to do this well. A directive style is characterized by one-way communication in which you are making clear what is expected, coaching on how to complete tasks, orienting to processes, etc. This is the style practiced for new employees or when new tasks are assigned to employees in order to get them off on the right foot.

If, like me, being direct is not a strong point for you, then you must be very conscious and deliberate to be sufficiently clear and complete with new employees or in assigning new responsibilities. Not having a strong directive style has resulted in my employees having to learn by making avoidable mistakes. I tend to assume that someone with the requisite experience or even aptitude can and will get it on their own. I regard being highly directive as an insult to someone with such a resume. I have learned the hard way, most notably through the story about the young clinic manager, David, that such assumptions are perilous.

So, I now begin orienting or "hatting" a new employee with the following disclosure: *"I need to forewarn you that I have a history of not doing well with starting employees off on a sound footing for success. I simply don't take the time or go to the needed depths in orienting to what is expected, what my standard for good performance is, what the relevant policies are and so on. I don't want to make that mistake with you. So, if I go into too much detail or cover something that you already know then I don't mean to insult your intelligence. I am just making sure that I don't make the mistakes I have made previously.*

Following the first few days of orienting or "hatting," it is likely that only Questions 1, 2 and possibly 4 & 5 are appropriate. But, give the employee the full list of questions and let him know you are going to want answers to the additional questions in the near future. You can jointly decide whether that should be 30, 60 or 90 days. My recommendation is that the shorter the waiting period, the better. This initial period is the key to developing a long-term, productive working relationship.

In completing organizational assessments for hundreds of organizations, often one of the priority issues for improved performance is improving the quality of employee orientation. Organizations and supervisors frequently don't do well setting up their own employees for success.

I would suggest having the conversation based on the 7 Questions early on as a way of evaluating whether orientation conducted by yourself and others has been adequate and how it can be improved. Introducing the questions at this juncture will make them less threatening later on when you are using them as part of an evaluation of your relationship with the employees.

2. Assessing the Quality of Supervision

As stated at the beginning of this chapter, if your employees are not increasingly adding value to the organization, then you are not doing your job as supervisor. Let me elaborate by reviewing each of the questions and look at how you might define specifics for improving your supervision.

1. Do You Know What's Expected of You?

A "no" response here could result from any of the following:

- Job description is unclear. It may be describing activities, but not the expected outcomes.
- Measures of success aren't defined.
- Priorities are unclear. It could be that you have sent signals verbally that create confusion as to what is important.
- Responsibilities in strategic planning or projects (i.e., specific projects outside of job description) are ill defined.
- Authorities for decision-making are not defined.
- Conflicting direction has come from one or multiple sources.
- The same assignments have been given to multiple individuals.

- There is lack of clarity regarding who is team leader on projects involving a team.
- Policies are unclear or inconsistently applied.

To get to clarity on what else might be needed, begin the dialogue with "What's missing?" or "What's unclear?" You need to be careful here. You may believe you have been very clear or you may somehow signal that you are offended when told that you have not been. Your body language can warn the employee to cease being truthful. Listen carefully. Get a precise definition of what's missing or unclear. Generalities in the employee's responses here are a sign of potential trouble (more on the "won't do" employee in the next chapter).

Based on the dialogue back and forth regarding what might be missing or needed, develop an action plan for correction. List the specific steps you need to take, prioritize them and commit to a date at which point you will have delivered the correction and checked to be sure that it is complete. Do this jointly with the employee, review the final product with him/her and then deliver a copy. Include in the action plan a periodic check on its progress, so you both can evaluate how it is going.

2. Do You Know What Good Performance Looks Like?

This question is about creating a clear picture of what standard or excellent performance on expectations looks like. These are your standards. Your experience has created a list of items that particularly please and annoy you in the results produced. What are those? Make them clear to your subordinate. That way she knows, before the game begins, what a homerun looks like in your eyes.

Remember the story about JoAnne, the office manager/consultant who was shocked to learn that excellence for me meant staying on the phone and being there for the customer rather than getting off as soon as possible? Be proactive; communicate these standards during orientation, so that you don't make the same mistake. Hidden standards pulled out at a later date make the employee wrong, are cause for a major upset and are hard to recover from.

3. Do You Get Feedback on the Results You Produce?

My take is that to get a "yes" that represents real certainty in the mind of your employee, the feedback has to be specific and should include both positive and negative comments. "Good job" simply doesn't get it. What was good about it? Or, what would it have taken to hear "great job?"

If you only provide feedback that is positive, the employee is going to question whether they are getting true or complete feedback. If you have previously communicated something like, "This was good, but would have been improved if ....," then when you do give unbridled positive feedback it is considered more genuine.

Most employees are harder on themselves than you will be. So, get rid of your reluctance to give negative feedback and commit to move to a fully honest and open relationship. Employees generally know when they are not performing well or up to their potential. They just don't know how negatively you judge their performance. Your feedback is almost certain to be good news relative to what they fear you will say.

You may also want to dialogue on whether your standards are reasonable or even correct. The customer for the employee's results (if someone other than you) may have told the employee that they want something else. Let's take the example of how JoAnne handled customer communications. There could be instances in which the customer has said, "I don't have time for chit chat. Just answer my questions as quickly as possible." The employee may have a better handle on shifts in customer (being that the customer is someone inside or outside the organization) needs and wants than you do.

Lastly, feedback is an ongoing, non-annual event. Evaluations or performance discussions should be done at least semi-annually and informal feedback should be ongoing. When you receive a work product from a direct report, give them feedback at that time. Was it great?

What would you suggest in the future that would make it even better? No feedback means you are not even acknowledging that the product is complete. This creates doubt as to whether the product matters, was worth the effort etc. In today's work environment, emails providing feedback can be sent quickly and easily.

4. Do You Have Sufficient Authority to Carry Out Your Responsibilities?

Situations that often arise surround the authority for hiring, rewarding and disciplining of employees. Not having complete authority would be like being held accountable to win the game when you aren't able to pick your own players or to bench bad performers.

Other areas to explore include authority over budget, authority to negotiate, authority to commit to contracts and the like.

You, as supervisor, may not have the authority yourself to deliver a "yes" on this question. But, knowing the negative impact that a lack of authority may be having on performance, you can advocate for expanded authority or rapid decisions from whoever does have the authority.

If there is insufficient authority, and you aren't able to grant additional authority or to deliver more rapid decisions, it may be that the expectations of the employee are unfair, i.e., mission impossible. If you judge that this is the case then you should re-negotiate the expectations.

5. Do you get timely decisions in the areas where you don't have authority?

Lack of authority (Question #4) usually means a waiting period for needed decisions. The delays may result in it not being possible to perform responsibilities or achieve expectations as your employee sees it. Delays also may suppress motivation and performance. This is an important area to discuss.

Failure to make needed decisions or make them in a timely manner is a major source of waste and lowered morale. So, if the answer is "no," then get clear on how this problem has impacted performance. Get the specifics as to what actually happened. Doing so may define opportunities for process improvement that could reap major benefits for the organization.

6. Do you have the data, resources and support needed to meet what is expected of you?

Rather straightforward here. If you get a "no," then a good follow-on question might be, "What additional information, resources or support would have enabled you to be more productive and successful?"

Repeating my previous word of caution, there is always pressure for more resources. Rarely, have I encountered a situation in which someone says, "I have all the employees and resources that I need." The pressure to increase budgets is constant. The ideal situation is a lean organization that is running resources hard, but not too hard. It is a tough line to find. Organizations that are fat become lethargic and don't perform well. Organizations that are too lean tend to create stress and they burnout their employees who question whether it will ever end. Finding the right mix of resources and expectations is challenging.

7. Do you get credit for the good results that you produce?

Getting an honest answer here will be challenging. At the root of this question is an employee admitting that they have need for this, which some may be reluctant to admit. Additionally, telling a supervisor that they don't give enough praise or credit is highly personal and a "no" response is almost a complaint about the character of the supervisor. Lastly, remember that "credit" is both praise and recognition for good results as well as compensation for the value that the employee adds. You may need to introduce the notion that you know this is difficult to talk about, but that you also know from your own experience that not feeling appreciated has an impact on motivation and thus performance.

3. Evaluating Employee Performance

As usually practiced, the normal annual evaluation process does not add value and can do damage. Evaluations tend to be one way conversations that focus on placing numerical scores towards vague questions that are intended to apply to every job. They are also largely subjective and don't lead to an effective game plan involving both the employee and supervisor that is designed to achieve an improved performance. Everyone dreads them, yet they are persistently used.

Because annual evaluations are generally one-way conversations, the supervisor is seen as sitting in judgment of the employee. An improved version of this is to have the employee complete a self-evaluation and compare the scores. Usually, employees are harder on themselves than the supervisor, which facilitates the conversation being a bit more positive and supportive. However, what is lacking here is the absence of an evaluation of whether the supervisor can improve his or her efforts to improve the performance of the employee.

I propose to replace this practice with more frequent conversations around the 7 Questions and to divorce the conversation from discussion of bonuses and the like. The conversations should focus on how the supervisor can truly add value by improving the performance of the employee.

One of my clients replaced the traditional annual evaluation and consideration of compensation with a conversation using the 7 Questions. That change alone totally shifted the organizational culture. What was anxious and negative about evaluations became a positive experience. Both supervisors and employees reported a great sigh of relief to have this negative experience removed. The annual conversations have led to both improvements in employee performance and in supervisory practice.

4. Determining the Proper Course of Action for the Underperforming Employee

The 7 Questions enumerate the responsibilities that you have as a supervisor for the development and support of good performances by your employees. So, in essence, if you have gotten a genuine "yes" to all 7 Questions and the employee is still not meeting performance standards, then, on some level, the employee has chosen to fail. In short, you are not the cause or contributor to the poor performance.

It has been my experience that all but the most ruthless of supervisors struggle to hold employees responsible for their poor performances. Some just struggle to sit in judgment of others. They don't want to be labeled as judgmental. Others rationalize that we are all human and struggle with life. All seem to ponder, "Is there something more that I should have done?" As long as they are still debating that question, they don't confront the employee and then the poor performance continues on.

The 7 Questions are intended to give you certainty that the proper course of action, at this point, is to hold the <u>employee</u> accountable for the Won't Do problem. To get to that certainty, try the following:

Meet with the employee and begin with a statement regarding your dissatisfaction with their level of performance. If you have not talked about their level of performance before, then apologize for not having done so (I concur with Blanchard that the feedback should be given to the employee as soon as possible after their poor performance has been identified. In his book, <u>The One Minute Manager</u>, he calls this feedback the "One Minute Reprimand"). Be as specific as possible (task, event and date what exactly was not up to standard) in your feedback.

If the employee gets defensive or wants to get into their explanation of the "whys" of the poor performance, ask them to hold off because you will be asking for that information in a moment (i.e., the 7 Questions are designed to pinpoint the "whys"). Then, explain that you want to identify what is contributing to their poor performance and that you will be employing a series of questions to try and identify the reason.

Then, go through the 7 Questions. If you get a "no" or a "well, I guess so," then ask for specifics as to what could have been provided by you that would have made a difference. Remember to use the follow-on questions in the "How to Get to 'Yes'" section of the chapter for the relevant question.

Beware of the employee that speaks in generalities. You may hear, "Well, everybody is confused," or "I'm just doing what everyone else does," or "We all have questions," etc. These statements are attempts to avoid accountability. In short, they are intended to keep you pondering that question, "What else could I have done to prevent this?"

If you insist on specifics, the employee may go into guilt or shame and take on the characteristics of a victim in an effort to ward off identifying the true causal factors. Express the fact that shame will do nothing to improve the performance. What is done is done. The question now is where we go from here. The employee may even attempt to build you up as part of this shameful response with statements about how understanding and patient you have been and so on. Again, this may be a tactic to gain your leniency and avoid responsibility.

Insist on going through the 7 Questions as a check to assure that something has not been missed in supporting good performance by the employee. Documenting the employee responses is sound practice here in case the employee files some sort of grievance against your actions as a supervisor.

Obviously, if there are legitimate specifics identified as you go through the questions, actions to get to a "yes" need to be defined and carried out by you as part of the solution.

If you have gotten a "yes" to all the questions or you are getting generalities as to why the response is "no," the conversation then might continue as follows:

Supervisor: I appreciate your honesty in answering the questions. What concerns me is that having gotten a "yes" to all the questions (or no specifics as to what else you need to do to get to a "yes"); I am at a loss as to what I can do to improve your performance. I want to be clear that at this point, your performance is not up to standard or what is needed from your position. The specifics of where you are failing are.................... Do you have any questions about that? Have we missed anything that I could have done to prevent the substandard performance you have contributed as of late?

Employee: Really, I don't know.

Supervisor: Are there factors at home or elsewhere in your life that explains what's going on?

Employee: Well, yes, ...

Supervisor: Well, it is your responsibility to handle these. I am happy to give you time off to handle them or support your getting any help that you may need, but we can't continue to have these conditions justify the performance we are experiencing.

Regardless of what form of help the employee may need, a firm and tightly managed plan of action holding the employee accountable for performance should be put in place. Elements of the plan might include: A formal warning, weekly performance targets, weekly check-in on whether targets are met and clarity that failure to meet those targets will result in termination.

Weekly performance targets should address areas where performance has been lacking. They could include attendance, due dates on assignments, responsiveness to communications or stepped up productivity, such as sales calls or patients seen.

In training supervisors, the most common natural or default style is one of a supportive leader, as it is known in the Situational Leadership II® model. When faced with a performance problem, supportive leaders instinctively respond with more two-way supportive communication or encouragement to overcome what the employee asserts to be the root causes of their poor performance. Often times, these "root causes" are factors outside of work, e.g., challenges with spouse or child, relatives needing attention and so on. Blanchard calls this "management by prayer."

Remember, when the root causes are within the domain of the workplace, they likely will surface in the form of a "no" response to one of the 7 Questions. Exceptions to this might be factors, such as perceived harassment or lack of cooperation from fellow employees. In both these cases, further investigation is needed to determine if the alleged root cause conditions must be remedied by the supervisor or whether these are put forth to deflect responsibility from the employee.

Upon further investigation, if the root cause is the responsibility of the employee, then a supervisory course of action that involves only more support absolves the employee of responsibility for the poor performance. The supervisor is taking responsibility for that failure and continues to tilt at windmills trying to find a magic formula to get the employee back on track.

Root causes that are likely the responsibility of the employee might include the following: Lack of dependable child care, problems with spouse, inability to cooperate with co-workers, substance abuse, car problems, public transportation problems and family problems.

I will focus a bit more on underperformers in the next chapter, Troubleshooting. To round up using the 7 Questions as a supervisor, note that your goal is to partner with your employees until there are honest "yes" answers to each question. And, once the "yeses" are in place, you can work toward making sure your employees continue to be able to answer "yes" and add value to your organization.

8. TROUBLESHOOTING

THERE ARE OTHER forces at work that will impact whether you receive truthful answers to the questions and are able to develop a plan of action that deals with the true causes of a "no" answer by yourself or your employee.

The following are some troubleshooting tips to help ensure that you get to the truth and to an effective plan of action.

A. The "Yes Man"

There will be a tendency for the employee to answer "yes" to each question. The tendency comes from not wanting to complain or upset the supervisor. Honest dialogue with authority figures is not something that employees have a lot of experience in. After all; responding truthfully to the questions will likely make them uncomfortable.

Factors contributing to a false "yes" may include not wanting to be a complainer, believing that the corporate culture rewards the tough who just find a way to "get 'er done" despite obstacles, or sensing that the supervisor really doesn't want to know and may punish the employee if given the truth.

If you sense that the employee is uncomfortable with the questions, go back to introduce the concept of partnering for performance (review "Set the Context" on page 30). Make it clear that you are using the questions to identify which part <u>each</u> of you can play towards getting to improved performance and job satisfaction.

Instruct the employee that when they consider each question, if the answer is "yes," but it could have gone better and should for the next employee, then they should answer with "no" or "somewhat," so you can be clear on how to improve.

Asking for advice on how you can get the next person in that position towards success may be a way to bypass the reluctance of the employee from being honest. After all, they are not "complaining" about what was or was not done to them. They are just giving advice for the future.

For example, if the employee is not clear on what is expected, could orientation of the policies have been improved? Is leadership practice sending a signal on what is important that is different than what was understood from the job description? Is leadership practice actually eroding the authority of the employee by second-guessing decisions or penalizing mistakes?

Even if the employee answers "yes," there is value in asking the additional questions detailed in each chapter to gain greater understanding.

B. Those Who Choose to Fail

Employees that don't perform despite all the steps that we have outlined in previous chapters largely fall into two categories: **1)** those that can't face the personal issues which only they can fix and **2)** those whose previous experiences have taught them that the only survival strategy at work is to create chaos around them in order to avoid accountability.

There is a smaller third category involving those lacking the confidence to take on a new challenge or to move on to acting independently on a task that you have been coaching them on. This third category can be addressed using the 7 Questions and development of a sound action plan to move them forward. It is rather like the difficult transition of getting a child to ride their bike without the training wheels. It is not done without risk, but ultimately, must be done for the child to succeed.

Now, let's address the two main groups for whom the 7 Questions and action plan to improve supervision, training and coaching won't do the trick.

1. Those with Personal Issues

This first category is self-explanatory. These are the employees trying to deal with divorce, loss of loved ones, chronic health issues, addiction issues, etc. The inability to face these issues will bleed into their work while resulting in a loss of motivation, inability to focus, inability to confront or inability to be honest with their self or others. This may be temporary, but it needs to be confronted early by the supervisor.

The strategy best employed for this group can best be described as "tough love." It is a combination of compassion and accountability based on the theory that the employee needs something to stabilize their life. They need some aspect of their life to feel good about and getting work performance back on track can be that opportunity. Ultimately, the choice to change has to be made by the employee. Employing the 7 Questions can get them to see that it really is their choice, which is to take responsibility and to choose wisely.

Doing this is challenging, indeed. Employees with personal issues often can't afford to lose their job or add to their existing problems, which is the poor performance problem you are insisting that they face. However, it is my experience that they already know in their heart of hearts that they are not performing and they already are not feeling good about it. Employing "tough love" to get them to feeling good about performance will strengthen them and provide a foundation from which they can better face the other issues in their lives.

2. Those Creating Chaos

It is this second category that is troublesome while giving supervisors fits and sleepless nights. It is because these individuals are a mystery that is clouded in false enthusiasm for work and a false positive attitude. They are tough to spot and tough to confront.

An Exemplifying Story

I first came across this over 20 years ago when working with an insurance group. The group had been in chaos for some time, but couldn't figure out why or find a solution.

I noticed as we went through the day that the most vocal member of the group kept challenging my questions. She was speaking for others and kept preventing the group from getting consensus on "what is." Whenever the discussion came to a specific point, she moved back to a generality or offered an exception to what was being said. Because she had been with the company the longest, she kept bringing up history that others were not familiar with. She was using information, hidden from others in the group, to divert the group from a solution. The group deferred to her because in the culture of the organization, she owned the history, experience and the "I am committed" card. No one would challenge her for these reasons.

I was experiencing the frustration that the group had been experiencing. As the day went on, I began to push back to ask for specifics. What data? Why specifically would this not work? She began to back down. The feeling in the room grew dark, indeed. The group grew increasingly anxious as they perceived that the "mother hen" was under attack. As the day ended, it was clear that only one of us, i.e., she or me, would survive the next day.

Well, it turned out that she arrived at work about an hour early the next day, having commuted an hour from her house to get there. She must have thought about it all night and on the drive. I think she saw the handwriting on the wall, so her game was going to be up if I continued my line of questioning in front of the group. Not wanting to be exposed, she chose to write a letter of resignation and put it on the director's desk before the session began.

Initially, the group was in shock and dismay. They could not see how they could go on without her as they went to her for all the answers. Well, it turns out they not only did fine without her, they prospered. After getting through all the emotions for the first hour or so, the group went on to effectively problem solve throughout the course of the day and then prospered from that point forward.

I had not seen this phenomenon before, but have seen it many times since. The ability such individuals have to keep co-workers and a supervisor wrapped around the axle is something to behold. Because of the confusion that is created, the supervisor can't get to a solution. It is like driving in a blinding fog. You just can't see clearly enough to proceed. So, you don't.

An Analogy to Explain

To better understand this group, let me offer an analogy. If you are attempting to train someone who has experienced nothing but losses in their education to date, you will have a very hard time being successful. Losses in education arise from the embarrassment of not having the answer when called on by the teacher, getting low test scores, being held back a grade, not getting into gifted and talented programs, or the student comparing him or herself with fellow students and judging themselves to be less intelligent.

Students with such experiences will avoid the training (out sick, family emergency, schedule conflicts) in order to avoid another loss. Or, they will attend the training but not offer questions. Instead, they will pretend that they are getting it and appear to be the model student. Rather than focusing on learning the material, they are focusing on avoiding attention of the punisher, which in this case is the teacher. They will summarize and state back what the teacher has said, so they appear to be a model student without ever really internalizing the information or thinking about how it might apply to their job/life. Therefore, they never learn it. They are just the teacher's pet, but at the end of the day they cannot and will not apply the learning because they have simply not learned it. Rather than getting smarter, the student falls further behind. Not wanting to continue to experience losses, they either avoid education or find ways to pretend they are getting it. It's a coping mechanism. Thus, they appear to be something they are not. I relay this example as everyone may have experienced a student such as this in their education journey.

How to Identify

A similar pattern exists with some employees. They appear to be saying and doing all the right things, but when you examine their results, they are not up to standard. These employees appear energetic, busy and committed. They speak up at meetings and are often looked up to by others, i.e., they are informal opinion leaders. But, if you carefully examine the statistics of their work, they are not getting results and they are committing numerous errors. There are always explanations for these lapses. Because they appear to be so committed, supervisors do not confront them. The excuses and apologies for the errors are accepted and the non-performance continues.

Another phenomena is that the teams that work with these folks are often in confusion and don't perform well for reasons they can't explain. With such individuals on a team, problem solving is never a linear process. Instead, the problem is the employee interjects tangential, often imagined causal factors that derail or delay the problem solving. They are seeking to avoid accountability by not being found out. In the end, the team simply can't make it go right, but can't explain why.

As in the education analogy, the source of this is previous losses. Either because of honest mistakes or bad supervision, the employee has been brutalized. They are convinced that they cannot get it right, so the strategy they employ is the avoidance of responsibility. They may not be conscious of it, but they don't believe they can succeed. So, it becomes about looking good rather than doing good.

An Important Distinction

I want to distinguish those creating chaos from those who don't want the training wheels taken off, i.e., don't want to act independently on a responsibility they have been given that you have been coaching them on.

For both groups, the root cause may be that they have been punished for mistakes in the past. The employee who lacks confidence is much easier to handle than the employee who has experienced so much loss, which means their only strategy at this point is to avoid responsibility. Those lacking confidence can be rehabilitated, if you will, by encouragement and the equivalent of a hand on their shoulder as the child takes his first ride without the training wheels. That is, you will break the fall or prevent a mistake from being made.

An Approach

The handling for those seeking to create chaos and avoid accountability is challenging. One should employ the 7 Questions but you will likely never get a "yes" to all 7 Questions if they know in the end, that the judgment will be that the fault lies with them.

Folks in this group seek to maintain confusion. Hence, they are never quite clear and that lack of clarity, which is your responsibility, is offered as the cause for the substandard performance. They will avoid ascribing the lack of clarity to something you as supervisor have failed to do (too easily corrected). Rather, you may hear something like:

- *Well, I thought that _____ (likely another employee or department) was responsible for that."*
- *"_____ communicated to me that we should wait before proceeding."*
- *"_____ said they wanted to handle it."*
- *"That directive was not clear to me and I wasn't sure who was responsible."*

The blanks will be filled either by a generality or an unidentifiable group. There will be an avoidance of naming an individual because it would be too easy to simply ask the named individual to learn that no such communication ever occurred. In short, these individuals will speak in generalities.

So, when employing the 7 Questions, you will need to be persistent in nailing down just exactly what the source of the confusion was, who said what, etc. If not, the process of you continuing to fill in the imagined gaps in your supervision in pursuit of a "yes" response will go on forever. You will be tilting at windmills.

You may be tempted to excuse the poor performance because of the exuberance and commitment to work that is communicated. This is the trap that supervisors find difficult to escape. The 7 Questions are designed to penetrate the camouflage and reveal to all that the solution lies with the employee and not the supervisor.

How to Handle Those Who Choose to Not Perform

Here's a list of steps to handle the Won't Do employees:

1. Confront the situation early. That may seem obvious and simple, but given that this person may well show up as your most loyal team member, it can be challenging. You have to focus on the data from actual results and not the behavior or spoken word.

2. Begin the discussion with, *"I have noticed that things aren't going well lately and I want to get this sorted out. To do this I want to go through a checklist of my responsibilities to provide you the clarity and support that you need to be successful. I want to be certain and specific as to what I need to do to get this turned around."* This will be met with shock by the news that it is not going well. There will be a challenge to provide data on specifics on the non-performance. Be prepared to deliver those specifics.

3. There may very well be an emotional outburst based on their loyalty and commitment to you. They will feel betrayed that you have judged them for not performing. You will need to get through that outburst and respond with the specifics on what was not done or not done well.

4. Each specific may then be challenged. You will need to reinforce the employee's responsibility for a given goal or task because confusion about that will be used as a defense. You will need to adjudicate what is confusion and what is the avoidance of responsibility for results.

5. If you decide that, in fact, you were not clear and that this contributed significantly to the non-performance, provide whatever information/training/direction is needed to get to a "yes" in an action plan.

6. Do not delay putting the employee on a very tight watch for task completions. State that you want to start fresh while addressing whatever contributed to the lack of clarity in the past. Go to a one-week task list that is tightly defined.

7. Meet at the end of each week and go over the results. You will quickly see either **a)** a pattern of improved performance or **b)** continued avoidance of responsibility for poor results.

8. If you are witnessing avoidance, then quickly communicate that it is your judgment that the employee is choosing to fail. There will be protest, again about confusions etc. But, if you look carefully the confusions will be communicated only at the moment of accountability rather than when you asked the 7 Questions.

9. This game can go on forever if you let it. Ask yourself, what responsibility is the employee taking his or herself to gain clarity either from you or from co-workers? Because supervisors tend to beat themselves up for the non-performance, employees in this category can be very successful in masking the truth and having these games go on forever.

I have seen entire organizations wrapped around the axle by these folks. It is important that you diagnose this problem early on and proactively nip it in the bud. If you follow the process I have outlined, you should be able to sleep at night when you offer to the individual that the situation is simply not working out and that both of you need a fresh start, i.e., the employee needs to move on to another organization.

An Instructive Success Story

Early in my career, my natural and virtually only style of leadership was to be supportive and encouraging. You can read that into the stories associated with each of the questions. In almost all cases, the failure on my part was a failure to deliver sufficient direction, be it the initial training or steps to reprimand poor performance.

After several years of frustration from tilting at windmills, I was a witness to the success of one of my directors who employed a very different approach. Jeannette was a nurse by training and a compassionate soul. But, she had an aversion for enabling dysfunction and poor performance from her direct reports. She appropriately focused on the needs of the organization for good performance. At the first sign of problems, she would confront the employee and encourage correction of the problem. She was generous with her time to meet with the employee and assured that all the aspects of supervision defined in the 7 Questions were addressed. If the deficiency was something she could address via training, coaching, encouragement, she was all over it.

Jeannette had a real nose for sensing when she was being played. If the employee was not doing his or her part, not putting forth the same effort that Jeannette was employing, then she would swiftly change course. She would confront the employee with the truth of not meeting their end of the bargain. She would put in place a very tight action plan to get the performance corrected. She would maintain her commitment of time to direct and support good performance, but only if the targets in the action plan that she had developed were met.

Her action plans would include the following: **a)** a formal warning that failure to meet the agreed upon elements of the action plan would constitute grounds for termination, **b)** absolute adherence to being on time to work, **c)** enrollment in counseling or a substance abuse program if needed, **d)** weekly deadlines, **e)** weekly meetings to review whether all conditions were met.

She set the standard for tough supervision in the organization. There was a blowback and she became known as "Mac the Knife" (a popular song at the time) for terminating those with performance problems. This aspect of her reputation was hurtful, but she was not deterred. I admired her courage and watched with keen interest to see the final outcomes. In virtually all cases, she was successful.

Success took two forms. A fair percentage of those she confronted were able to turn things around and sustain good performance going forward. They were grateful for the wakeup call. Those that were not able to turn it around were terminated. In each case, she would be in my office in tears wondering whether she had done the right thing or not. In most cases, there were circumstances outside of work, mostly family problems, which were impacting the employee. A woman of compassion, Jeannette was challenged to hold the line in these circumstances. But, often, several months down the road, the former employee would converse with Jeannette and communicate something along these lines. "At the time you let me go, I hated you. But after several months, I realized that you made me look at what I was doing to myself, and I have since turned my life around. Thank you."

The conversations Jeannette would have when putting in place a strict plan of action would go something like this:

Supervisor: I know that you have challenges outside of work that are making it difficult for you to focus on work. But right now, you need to feel good about something in your life. That is the only way you will have the strength to turn your life around. What you can control is what happens here at work and I want you to feel good about your performance. You performed well before and you can do so again. So, I am going to put in place a very strict plan that holds you accountable. We will start with small steps and then work our way back to good overall performance. We will agree to each of the elements of this plan. As long as you are meeting your commitments, then I will continue to do all that I can to support you in being successful. If you don't meet each and every element of the plan, then I will terminate you."

Tough love indeed, but proven to be successful. Witnessing this changed my perspective on supervision dramatically. I worked hard at becoming more direct. I would counsel new employees that being direct enough is something that I struggle with and asked them to assist me by letting me know when the genuine answer to any of the 7 Questions was "no." Over time, I became a much better supervisor.

Both Jeannette's story and my own journey taught me that honesty is the key to good supervision. In their heart of hearts, employees know that they are not performing well and that it is their responsibility. They may react when confronted with it, but time after time, I have been thanked for being honest. Often, I have been told that they thought I was going to be more upset than I was. I cannot say that I ever found this easy, but I know that being honest is in the best interest of both the organization and the employee.

A Final Word on Those Choosing to Fail

As a final point here, I would note that coming to a judgment that someone is willfully (consciously or unconsciously) creating chaos to avoid accountability may fly in the face of your core beliefs. You simply can't get yourself to judge someone that harshly. I know this has been challenging for me. But, having been played by such individuals and seeing other executives suffer the same has convinced me that this phenomena still exists. My advice would be to separate your judgment of performance from the judgment of the individual. The poor performance and their responsibility for it is what are true at this point in time. It is likely not who they want to be. You're calling a halt to the game that you both are playing, which serves you and them best in the long run because it enables both sides to make better choices.

It is not my intent to demonize this group. They may very well have been victims of former bad supervision just as the failing student may be the victim of bad teachers. But, that does not justify this from continuing on. The question is what to do about it. Enabling them serves no end. They continue having to pretend rather than to perform, which causes them to continually come up with new defense mechanisms and confusions. The question is, with the truth on the table, what choice do they wish to make? Continuing to fool themselves and others may be that choice, but just don't let it be your choice.

9. SOME FINAL THOUGHTS

As DISCUSSED IN Chapter 2, most managers simply don't give management work enough time or attention, hence the "management gap" that Lewis Allen talked about. The legendary CEO of ITT, Harold Gineen, referred to the same problem in his book Managing[4], when he wrote, "managers must manage."

Well, why the "gap" and why don't they manage? Allen found that managers choose to do technical work if given a choice because that's their experience and proven expertise. It is what they are trained in and know best. Managers are often chosen because they are the best at their technical work. The belief is that somehow their expertise will get instilled in their workers via osmosis. But, management work involves an entirely different set of skills, and often technical experts are thrust into it with no training in these new skills whatsoever.

Other reasons managers prefer technical work is that getting a tangible outcome from management work takes more time, is less certain and, lastly, involves dealing with people problems that are more difficult than technical challenges. Sound familiar?

My hope in writing this book is that I have aided you in closing your personal "management gap" and that the 7 Questions will make it easier for you to face, dialogue and plan with subordinates. I also hope that you come to realize the immense satisfaction that can come from growing those who work for you. Despite the challenges of management work, doing it well can be the ultimate satisfaction.

As you look back on your career, yes, promotions would have been nice and hitting goals would have been gratifying. But, my take is that

---

4   Gineen, H., Managing, Doubleday, 1984

you will most value seeing those who work for you succeed. The success of others will be the ultimate success for you.

APPENDIX

The Seven Questions

Supervisor:

Instructions: Please answer "yes" or "no" to each of the following questions. In considering your answer, look as to whether you are receiving the information from your supervisor vs. determining for yourself. If you are not sure of your answer, then answer "no".

1. Do you know what is expected of you? ❑Yes ❑No

2. Do you know what good performance looks like in your job as defined by your supervisor? ❑Yes ❑No

3. Do you get feedback on the results that you produce?
    ❑Yes ❑No

4. Do you have sufficient authority to carry out your responsibilities?   ❑Yes ❑No

5. Do you get timely decisions in the areas where you don't have authority?   ❑Yes ❑No

6. Do you have the data, resources and support needed to meet what is expected of you?   ❑Yes ❑No

7. Do you get credit for the good results that you produce?
    ❑Yes ❑No

Sample Purposes

For Director of Sales
To create revenue to maintain future viability and growth.

For Information Technology
To establish and maintain information management systems that support productivity and effective decision-making within the company.

For HR
To assure that; a) the organization has sufficient staff to support effective operations, b) all persons employed or contracted by the company are well and properly placed in service, and each one's forward progress as a staff member is uninterrupted and c) management of personnel conforms to applicable state and federal laws/regulations.

Sample Products

For Director of Sales
- A well-trained, effective sales force.
- Campaigns to generate interest in continuing to do business with our organization are designed and implemented.
- Sales data on customers and prospective customers are maintained and understood by all staff.
- Policies in place and followed to support effective sales function.

For Information Technology
- Effective I.T. strategy defined and updated that maintains cutting edge position relative to competitors
- Hardware & software needs of the organization are addressed to ensure cost effective and efficient operations.
- Policies and procedures established that maintain effective and efficient I.T. practices.
- Staff literate in I.T. applications, so it does not hamper performance.

For HR
- Budgeted positions filled with competent, qualified personnel.
- New personnel understand company philosophy, principles, policies, benefits and expectations.
- Employee records are maintained.
- Performance management and compensation systems maintained.
- All benefits received by eligible employees.
- Effective employee training and development program carried out.
- All applicable laws and regulations are adhered to and personnel policies remain current.
- Supervisors coached on handling personnel matters.
- Employee grievances adjudicated.
- Internal staff publication produced monthly.

Sample Statistics

For Director of Sales
- Gross revenue scheduled
- Gross revenue profitability of jobs
- Opportunities lost

For Information Technology
- Computer down time, service interruptions
- Technical assistance work requests
- Trainings conducted

For HR
- # open positions
- Time to fill vacancies
- Grievances filed
- # trainings delivered

ABOUT THE AUTHOR

 WILLIAM DANN BEGAN with a 13-year career in management, out of which 9 of those years was spent as CEO. He launched his consulting business in 1981 with a passion for enabling organizations and individuals to reach their fullest potential. During those early years of consulting, he also taught management at the graduate level for six years at Boston University.

His company, Professional Growth Systems LLC, has served over 200 organizations in the U.S. and abroad using proprietary solutions developed by his team that accelerate performance with as little time and resources as possible. Throughout his career, he has continued to focus on improving the methods that spark innovation while overcoming resistance to change. He has also served as a coach to a number of CEO's.

In *Creating High Performers* he lays out his own learning about how to develop those you work with and to do it with certainty.

Bill writes two newsletters each month, one on management and the other on governance. He also maintains a blog on management and related topics. He is the founder of BoardGrowth.com , a web-site devoted to advancing the effectiveness of governing boards.

Bill and his wife, Jenny, live in Anchorage, Alaska with son, Tyler and his family, including two grandchildren close by.

To subscribe to his newsletters and read his blog, visit
http://www.professionalgrowthsystems.com/
You can also connect with Bill on LinkedIn (William Dann)
or Twitter
https://www.twitter.com/arcticwill

CPSIA information can be obtained
at www.ICGtesting.com
Printed in the USA
FSOW04n1039040615
7643FS